RULES OF THUMB FOR ONLINE RESEARCH

RULES OF THUMB FOR ONLINE RESEARCH

DIANA ROBERTS WIENBROER
Nassau Community College

Boston Burr Ridge, IL Dubuque, IA Madison, WI
New York San Francisco St. Louis
Bangkok Bogotá Caracas Lisbon London Madrid Mexico City
Milan New Delhi Seoul Singapore Sydney Taipei Toronto

McGraw-Hill Higher Education

*A Division of The **McGraw-Hill** Companies*

RULES OF THUMB FOR ONLINE RESEARCH

Published by Irwin/McGraw-Hill, an imprint of The McGraw-Hill Companies, Inc. 1221 Avenue of the Americas, New York, NY, 10020. Copyright © 2001 by Diana Roberts Wienbroer. All rights reserved. No part of this publication may be reproduced or distributed in any form or by any means, or stored in a data base or retrieval system, without the prior written consent of The McGraw-Hill Companies, Inc., including, but not limited to, in any network or other electronic storage or transmission, or broadcast for distance learning.

Some ancillaries, including electronic and print components, may not be available to customers outside the United States.

This book is printed on acid-free paper.

2 3 4 5 6 7 8 9 0 DOC/DOC 0 9 8 7 6 5 4 3 2 1 0

ISBN 0-07-236684-2

Editorial director: *Phillip A. Butcher*
Senior sponsoring editor: *Lisa Moore*
Editorial assistant: *Robyn Catania*
Marketing manager: *Thayne Conrad*
Project manager: *Rebecca Nordbrock*
Production supervisor: *Heather Burbridge*
Freelance design coordinator: *Pam Verros*
Supplement coordinator: *Nathan Perry*
New media: *Todd Vaccaro*
Compositor: *Shepherd Incorporated*
Typeface: *10/12 Palatino*
Printer: *R. R. Donnelley & Sons Company*

Library of Congress Cataloging-in-Publication Data
Wienbroer, Diana Roberts.
    Rules of thumb for online research/Diana Roberts
Wienbroer.
        p. cm.
    ISBN 0-07-236684-2 (alk. paper)
    1. Online data processing. 2. Information retrieval.
3. Internet (Computer network) I. Title.

QA76.55. W54 2001
025.04--dc21   00-033920

www.mhhe.com

CONTENTS

PART 2: HOW TO ASSESS THE INFORMATION YOU HAVE FOUND

PART 3: TIPS FOR ORGANIZING YOUR PROJECT

PART 4: HOW TO DOCUMENT THE INFORMATION YOU USE

PART 5: A GUIDE FOR BEGINNERS 125

APPENDICES 149

Updated Internet addresses for this book can be found at McGraw-Hill's website: <http://www.mhhe.com/english>.

TO THE INSTRUCTOR

Rules of Thumb for Online Research is designed for students to use on their own while they are working at the computer. Chapters are organized sequentially within the five parts, but the parts may be used out of order, depending on the student's needs. This book can help students who just need facts from reliable sources and those who are working on sophisticated research projects.

The Basics Although most users of this book will already be familiar with computers, the Internet, and basic principles of research, some won't be. Part 5 provides essential operational information for students who might be inexperienced or confused about the most efficient ways to use a keyboard and mouse. In addition, students unfamiliar with computer terminology will find the definitions of key terms in the glossary, beginning on page 151.

Time/File Management Similarly, students often need help in managing their research projects. Part 3 advises students about organizing their time and the overwhelming amount of information they will find.

Conducting the Search *Rules of Thumb for Online Research* begins at the point where most students want to start: "Hop on the Internet." Part 1 describes how to use each Internet resource in order to gather the greatest amount of useful information. Following the sequence of Part 1 controls students' frustrations of finding too many (lightweight, commercial) and too few (substantial, suitable) results from an Internet search.

Assessing the Results Part 2 helps students evaluate and organize what they find online. This aspect of Internet research requires the most professional advice; it is the one topic of this book that implies classroom or conference support. Students can use the checklists provided on their own, but most will need the guidance of their instructor in interpreting the quality of information found at specific websites.

Documentation Part 4 provides the rules for documentation format. Detailed examples explain the MLA, APA, CBE, Chicago Manual, Columbia, ACS, and footnote/endnote styles for reporting research in an easy-to-understand, rules-of-thumb approach.

Internet Addresses The Appendix collates all the Internet addresses given throughout the book, plus many other recommended sites. From headings alone, the Appendix provides a guide to how the student might best proceed to find information on the Internet.

I hope that you find this guide helpful. All Internet addresses are current as of April 2000. If you have any comments or suggestions, please e-mail or write:

wienbrd@sunynassau.edu

Diana Roberts Wienbroer
English Department
Nassau Community College
Garden City, NY 11530

Acknowledgments

First and foremost, I want to thank my long-time writing partners, Elaine Hughes and Jay Silverman, who have supported me in this solo effort and in all our other collaborative work. Their approaches to the writing/research processes have helped me refine both my own processes and the specific elements of this book. Their comments on various drafts have been invaluable. However, their most significant contribution has been allowing me to use our collaboratively established title, *Rules of Thumb;* this streamlined approach to each topic has shaped every page.

In addition, I'm particularly grateful to Emily Hegarty, English Instructor at Nassau Community College, and Barbara Neilon, Librarian Emerita at Colorado College, for offering detailed commentary on the manuscript and much-needed questioning of key researching points. Generous advice from a number of other colleagues at Nassau Community College also influenced this book: Ed Blesch, Rebecca Fraser, and Jessica Yood in the English Department provided thoughtful comments and insights; the staff of the Academic Computer Services and all the reference librarians helped with technicalities; any mistakes are mine, not theirs.

Helen Collins (Professor Emerita, Nassau Community College), Jane Collins (Pace University), and Scott Zaluda (Nassau Community College) provided intelligent, thorough reviews of my earlier book, *The McGraw-Hill Guide to Electronic Research and Documentation,* which was the springboard for *Rules of Thumb for Online Research.* The earlier Guide would not have happened without the vision of Tim Julet and Phil Butcher at McGraw-Hill.

I'm also indebted to the other reviewers who pointed to areas that needed clarification. Their comments were both specific and encouraging.

- Dr. Paula J. Smith Allen (Southeastern Oklahoma State University)

- Anne Bliss (University of Colorado at Boulder)

- Dr. Gwen Chandler-Thompson (Florida Community College at Jacksonville)

- Elaine Freeman (Southeastern Oklahoma State University)

- Catherine Gouge (West Virginia University)

- Claudine Keenan (Penn State University)

- Linda Maifair (Wilson College)

- Myrna Nurse (West Virginia University)

- Kathryn M. Peterson (University of Houston)

- Susan Slavicz (Florida Community College)

- Marsha Spiegelman (Nassau Community College)

At McGraw-Hill, Senior Editor Lisa Moore has been especially supportive. Her insistence on the title helped me transform my earlier drafts into a much more accessible book. I also appreciate her many substantive suggestions on content. Editorial Assistant Emily Sparano smoothed many trails in the early days of the book's progress; then her successor, Editorial Assistant Robyn Catania, saw it through to the final stages of production. Project Manager Rebecca Nordbrock assured the careful attention to the spirit and letter of this book. They all have simplified my task considerably.

Finally, I want to thank my husband, Carl; our son, Kirtley; Evelyn Brooks; Leanna Fisher; Sarah Pond; Carolyn Roughsedge; and my students at Nassau Community College during the fall 1999 and spring 2000 semesters. All provided extensive feedback on how to meet the practical needs of online researchers in a variety of real-life conditions.

Other books in the *Rules of Thumb* Series:

Silverman, Hughes, and Wienbroer. *Rules of Thumb: A Guide for Writers,* 4th ed.

—. *Good Measures: A Practice Book to Accompany Rules of Thumb,* 4th ed.

—. *Rules of Thumb for Research.*

Wienbroer, Hughes, and Silverman. *Rules of Thumb for Business Writers.*

(All from McGraw-Hill copyright 2000, updated to include 1999 MLA guidelines. Some of the material in this book appeared in a different form in the above books.)

To the Student

You've been doing research since you were born—discovering how your own observations, thoughts, and feelings compare to those of others. One kind of research is just asking questions and evaluating the answers. This book can help with that basic element of curiosity as you use the Internet. However, more refined methods of research are used in academic and professional settings, usually resulting in a report or a public presentation.

Rules of Thumb for Online Research is designed to support you as you search for information on the Internet. This book will help you find information more quickly, evaluate its appropriateness for your needs, and then meet the format requirements for a report, whether in business or academic settings.

Rules of Thumb for Online Research is for you

- if you are a hacker or a beginner assigned to write a college research paper in any course.

- if you are in the working world and must find information to solve a problem or to include in a memo or formal report.

- if you're at home seeking information for personal decisions, for activities in your community, or to help a child with homework.

The topics in *Rules of Thumb for Online Research* can be referenced out of order, while you are working at the computer. I assume that most readers of this book are already familiar with computers, the Internet, and basic principles of research. In that case you're ready to start with Part 1. However, some of you may want to begin by reading the tips for beginners in Part 5 or the tips for planning the research project in Part 3. If you come across an unfamiliar term, you'll find the definition in the glossary beginning on page 151.

Part 1 explains how to gather information. It can be used one chapter at a time as you try different resources. **Part 2** helps you evaluate and organize what you have discovered. **Part 3** gives tips on methods of working and controlling your project. Turn to that section early if you're new to research, new to the Internet, or facing a close deadline. **Part 4** provides details on documentation format for the most commonly used styles for reporting research. **Part 5** gives tips for working with computers. A **glossary** and **all the Internet addresses for resources** mentioned throughout the book are in the **Appendix.**

This book is part of the *Rules of Thumb* series, which is designed to help people meet the requirements of writing assignments. The phrase "rule of thumb" refers to a handy guideline: The top part of your thumb is roughly an inch long. Sometimes you need a ruler, marked in millimeters, but often you can do fine by measuring with just your thumb. Your thumb takes only a second to use, and it's always with you. Similarly, a few basic rules for writing—our *Rules of Thumb*—will serve you for most assignments.

Updated Internet addresses for this book can be found at McGraw-Hill's website: <http://www. mhhe.com/writers>.

I hope that you find this guide helpful. All Internet addresses are current as of April 2000. If you have any comments or suggestions, please e-mail or write:

wienbrd@sunynassau.edu

Diana Roberts Wienbroer
English Department
Nassau Community College
Garden City, NY 11530

DEDICATION

To the users of this book: I hope that this guide simplifies your search.

RULES OF THUMB FOR ONLINE RESEARCH

PART 1

HOW TO FIND INFORMATION

FIND YOUR FOCUS

Whether you already have a topic or are facing an assignment where you have a choice of topic, spend some preliminary time either jotting down ideas and questions or browsing online.

■ FIND YOUR CONNECTION TO AN ASSIGNED TOPIC

Brainstorm

Brainstorming is jotting down your ideas without inhibitions. Just list your topic, and then write down questions and subtopics—whatever comes to mind—without worrying about correctness or relevance. This method gets to those ideas that lurk below those on the top of your head; and although some may not be workable, you should discover some that are worthwhile. Brainstorming for 7 to 20 minutes can show you where you would like to learn more.

It is always easier to do required research if your own curiosity motivates you. For example, if you have an interest in film and media, and your general topic is the Great Depression in the United States, your brainstorming might show you a manageable research topic: the effect of the Depression on the movie-making industry.

Browse Online to Find Your Subtopic

Another method is to go online and enter your general topic in a subject directory such as Yahoo <http://www.yahoo.com>. Click on some subtopics and visit a few websites to gather some possibilities.

For the Great Depression, a few mouse clicks in Yahoo could lead you to the University of Michigan's history museum site <http://www.sos. state.mi.us/history/museum/explore/museum>, where you would find a series of resources that explain what life was like for Americans living in the 1930s, including their radio and film interests.

■ FIND A TOPIC YOU CARE ABOUT

Brainstorm

You may have an assignment where you have total free choice. Let's say that you must write an article for a newsletter for a parents' organization. Making a list of topics that might interest your readers could lead you to a good topic—perhaps how to teach children to be skeptical about what they find on the Internet.

Browse Online to Find Your Subtopic

Instead of brainstorming, you might just hop on the Internet. You can find a topic by going to a subject index and clicking on the categories that apply to your audience or course. For example, for a required paper on contemporary American drama, you could do subject searches at Hotbot <http://www.hotbot.com>, AltaVista <http://www.altavista.com>, or Yahoo and click on the categories under "theater." Follow the subtopics and links until you find something that interests you. You could, for example, end up with a topic on how interactive and alternative theater groups are helping disadvantaged teenagers.

You can also check a subject directory on the Internet to see what categories are listed for your general interests. For example, suppose you have a love of animals and a vague idea that you will do some sort of report about the use of animals in medical research. A subject search at About.com <http://www.about.com> or Yahoo could take you pretty quickly to articles about the pregnant mares whose urine provides estrogen for the hormone replacement therapy that so many millions of women are now taking. This narrow topic could be thoroughly discussed in a research paper. In addition to discovering details about the treatment of the horses themselves, you could get related information on the pharmaceutical industry, statistics on the number of menopausal women taking the hormone produced this way, the alternatives in synthetic hormones, and what veterinarians say about stress on animals.

Whatever you select as a topic, be aware that your paper must ultimately develop a manageable subtopic. For example, you might be interested in divorce, but you will need to narrow your area of research—perhaps by looking at the effects of late divorce on adult children.

Identify Your Angle on the Subtopic

In addition to narrowing your topic to a subtopic, think of what area of emphasis you can use to focus your search. For example, a project studying drug and alcohol abuse could begin by narrowing the research to the study of one drug, but what would be the emphasis? Identify some questions you want answered. You might list several:

> What are the harmful effects on the individual, the family, the community?
>
> What treatments work?
>
> What are the current laws and conviction rates?
>
> What are the economic factors?

Use the question that interests you the most to help you decide what information you need.

Original topic → subtopic→ sub-subtopic

Drug abuse → cocaine abuse → the effects of long-term cocaine abuse

or   → the laws for crack and powder cocaine

or   → cocaine abuse among the poor and wealthy

Use Links
and Bookmarks

Some of the most valuable information on the
Internet comes from places where others have
sent you.

The Internet began as a means for scientists to
share information. That spirit still governs the best
of the Internet. Although commercial interests may
now seem to dominate, there are still an incredible
number of people who post material for others to
use—for free and in the spirit of openly sharing
information. This is the part of the Internet you can
tap into, to inform yourself and to participate in
public discourse.

The most important characteristic of the Internet
and more specifically the World Wide Web is
openness: it is democratic—and disorganized. You
can't predict what you will find. You may follow a
promising lead and find an article about your
topic—say the mystery writer Helen MacInnes—
but just as easily find the picture of someone's dog
named after Helen MacInnes.

■ Be Persistent

The first few research sessions should be for
exploring.

- Use search engines.

- Use the resources on the search engines'
  homepages.

- Use reference lists.

Don't give up when you get disappointing replies to your queries. Read this book to learn about your options: there are a number of different avenues to explore and different methods for asking questions.

Search engines by themselves will not be enough to help you find the information you seek, but the links from the sites that the search engines find will lead you—as long as you are persistent.

■ Bookmark the Links

During your first few research sessions, survey and bookmark each interesting page you visit. Bookmarking (saving the Internet address in your browser—called *history* in Netscape and *favorites* in AOL) is faster than writing down addresses or downloading files. To do so, just click on the "button" at the top of the screen—labeled *bookmark* in Netscape or Internet Explorer, *favorites* or the heart icon in AOL. Skim rapidly. Do a quick assessment of the quality of the information at a particular site, bookmark it if it seems worthwhile, and then move on to other sites that a particular search has turned up. This is the fastest way to get a sense of what information is available.

Then go back to those bookmarked sites and methodically determine which you definitely can use or might want to use again; save those Internet addresses to your disk, or e-mail them to yourself. Unfortunately, with most programs, you will have to copy and paste the addresses one at a time. If you are using a computer at your library or computer lab, make sure that you have all the information for each site before you finish your session. Other users will be bookmarking after you; some libraries erase the histories each evening.

Print entire files only if you really need a paper copy. Illustrations, for example, can be downloaded and saved on disk to be imported later into your document.

Remember that with many programs, you can only save or print the screens you're actually viewing. Ordinarily, you will need to bring up each link first before saving or printing it. If you have time, you can select out individual sections of those webpages you found useful. Otherwise, save the entire document to study later.

■ Be Uninhibited—At Least for a While

A research project should introduce you to new ways of viewing the topic, so plan your research process, not the outcome. If you think specifically about the organization and conclusions of the report too soon, you will block what should be an exploration, an openness to new ideas. Stay open to discovering new information and to interpreting old information in new ways.

For your first searches, you will benefit from exploring wherever the links take you. This quick surfing often leads to surprising and interesting material. Later, you can analyze what you've discovered. As long as you bookmark (and then save the bookmark list on a disk as backup), you will be able to revisit those sites.

SEARCH SUBJECT DIRECTORIES

Subject directories such as Yahoo and Magellan allow you to enter a search term or to click on topics, subtopics, sub-subtopics, and so forth.

The advantage of searching by subject is that a professional researcher has assembled the answers. Subject directory databases are actually organized indexes. Your search terms are matched against a list of terms that have been set up by someone who knows the field and who has read the articles in the database. Thus your results will usually be relevant to what you ask for.

For example, you could enter the subject "distance education" in the query box in Yahoo <http://www.yahoo.com>, or you could click on "education," then "university/college" and then "distance learning." Either way, you would find an alphabetical listing of colleges and universities that offer distance learning programs. Seeing the word "telecourse," you might try entering that word in the query box. Yahoo would then provide you with a definition of "telecourse" and a listing of institutions offering telecourses with links to each.

You would get a different list of websites if you used AltaVista's subject directory; in addition, at AltaVista <http://www.altavista.com> you would find a different subcategory, "online education," with links to colleges offering courses on the Internet.

At Magellan <http://magellan.excite.com>, the same subject search yields still different sites, and they are listed with brief descriptions and ranked by relevance to your subject "distance learning." Magellan also offers a link to Excite. Its search yields a link to the World Lecture Hall <http://www.utexas.edu/world/lecture> with links to faculty worldwide who have posted information on their courses.

So with a simple subject search, just a few mouse clicks can often get you a great deal of information very quickly.

See the appendix of this book for the addresses for other subject directories.

Use Reference Pages

Reference pages link you quickly to relevant resources often not found by search engines.

General reference pages are websites that provide links to key resources for basic research. There are also a number of reference pages organized around particular disciplines. For both these types, a researcher has posted links to a variety of sources of information, many of which would not be found by the search engines.

Find the Appropriate Reference Page for Your Topic

Reference pages are worth the sleuthing effort necessary to find them. Important reference pages are listed beginning on page 165.

Check the homepages of search engines. Almost all search engines offer comprehensive reference lists on their homepage.

Check Virtual Library. This site, <http://www.vlib.org/overview.html>, offers a vast list of resources—and each category is maintained by an expert in that field.

Look up faculty pages at colleges and universities. Professors routinely post their course materials, including links to libraries and other resources of information. You can find these pages through search engines. Try using the name of a particular college or your topic phrase plus "college or university."

The World Lecture Hall at the University of Texas <http://www.utexas.edu/world/lecture> posts links to faculty homepages, all over the world, by discipline. Many of these sites provide very detailed college course outlines, reading lists, and links to other resources.

Check library homepages; ask your librarian. More and more libraries are providing reference pages with excellent links. Don't limit yourself to your own library; check others as well. Addresses for major research libraries are listed on page 175.

Prepare Phrases for Your Searches

Most search tools allow you to type in a list of words for them to look for. You can give more precise directions by adding punctuation and connective words (Boolean operators) to create a search string.

■ Develop a List of Terms

Electronic searches are conducted by telling the computer what words or phrases to look for. You can make a list of subtopics and synonyms, or you can get some keywords by consulting an article in an encyclopedia, such as *The Free Internet Encyclopedia* <http://clever.net/cam/encyclopedia> or *Encyclopaedia Britannica* <http://www.britannica.com>. Alternatively, an encyclopedia may be part of your word-processing program or in the reference section of your online service.

Note that information in the encyclopaedia may not be appropriate for your paper; however, it can help get you started by providing you with some background information and with a list of specific terms to use for searching.

For example, an article in *Encyclopaedia Britannica* on "diabetes" used these terms:

diabetes mellitus
blood glucose level
diagnosis
endocrine system
soluble fiber

therapies
pancreas
disorder of carbohydrate
   metabolism

These terms can be used in several combinations when employing a search engine.

◼ DEVELOP QUESTIONS AND MAP OUT WHERE TO RESEARCH

Make a list of questions that you need the answers to. Some may be brief ones that can be answered by a single statistic, such as "How many American teenagers have diabetes?" But others might be more complicated, such as "How do diet and exercise relate to insulin needs?" When you get online, you will find that some search engines—AltaVista and AskJeeves, for example—allow you to ask a question in their query box.

Next think of who might know (and be willing to tell) the answers to your questions.

For example, you might list these possible sources for information on diabetes:

> doctors–endocrinologists
> nutritionists
> medical sites
> Diabetes Association

This list will help you identify the journals and websites you should consult, the names you should enter in searches, and perhaps the names of those to whom you could send an e-mail inquiry.

◼ USE PUNCTUATION AND BOOLEAN OPERATORS

Every search program uses slightly different rules of operation, but most use two searching conventions. Check the directions or helpline of the program before beginning.

- Quotation marks indicate that a phrase is to be treated as one search term—for example, "blood glucose."

- "Boolean operators" such as *and* and *or* tell the computer how to interpret your list of search terms. In general:

    and specifies that <u>both</u> terms should appear.

    or specifies that <u>either</u> term should appear.

    not specifies that a term <u>should not</u> appear.

When a search engine says that "Boolean *and* is implied," you don't need to type *and*; just type in all the terms you want with a space between them.

Some search engines use the plus sign (+) to mean that a particular term *must* appear, and the minus sign (−) instead of *not*.

For example, information on adolescent diabetes in humans (as opposed to cats) can be found with these search terms:

> "adolescent diabetes" and diet and exercise and insulin not cat not feline

or

> +"adolescent diabetes"+diet+exercise+
> insulin-cat-feline

■ USE VARIOUS COMBINATIONS OF SEARCH TERMS

Try to identify what you hope the articles you find will discuss. There may be a number of documents about your exact topic; but more likely, the articles will discuss one aspect or another—not all you want to know. Play with your list of possible terms and see what combinations work best with the search programs you are using.

NARROW YOUR SEARCH

To avoid finding too much information:

- Specify that two terms must appear—*newts and salamanders.*

- Use a long string of words—if your search engine allows it.

- Use several phrases *"corporate spying," "intellectual property," "computer security."*

- Exclude words or phrases. For example, for a search on computer security, specifying *not children, not parent* would eliminate articles discussing the parental control of their children's access to certain websites.

EXPAND YOUR SEARCH

If you narrowed your topic and can't get enough information, you may have to find it inside articles on more general or related topics. To make certain you have enough articles:

- Request alternatives—*dairy or milk or eggs or cream or cheese.*

- Submit synonyms—*green or "environmentally friendly" or "eco-safe".*

- Submit words instead of phrases—*corporate, espionage, patent.*

- Submit more general terms—instead of *cockatiel,* try *exotic birds.*

In spite of your best efforts, you may not find any sources or you may find hundreds of thousands. In either case, first think about what you asked and then rephrase your search.

IF THERE IS NO MATCH FOR YOUR REQUEST

- You may have misspelled one or more words.

- You may have used the wrong symbols or phrasing for that particular search engine. Consult the helpline.

- You may need to try a different search engine or database.

- Try alternatives. For example, if you specified *newts and salamanders,* change your query to *newts or salamanders.* Once you find some sites, their links will take you to others that may be more specific.

- Give both the abbreviation and the full name, linked by *or* —NPR or *"National Public Radio."*

- Try adding more alternatives— *Irish or Gaelic or Celtic.*

IF YOU HAVE TOO MANY LISTINGS

You may get enough information by reading the top articles listed. Ordinarily, if you get a great many listings, you shouldn't bother with more than the top 10 or 20 results in any case. The top articles on the list use your required terms more frequently and have been rated "most relevant" to the topic you have specified. After you read the twentieth one, you are unlikely to find much more information and are better off changing search terms or changing search engines.

- Take a look at the first 10 to see if they coincide at all with your topic. For instance, if your inquiry on diabetes yielded thousands of articles and most of them are personal stories from cat owners about feline diabetes, you'll need to rephrase the search string or use a different search engine.

- If the first 10 listings *are* on your topic, download a few of them to skim offline and extract more search terms to use.

- If the search engine allows it, add more technical or specific terms to your search string—*"adolescent diabetes" "blood glucose level" prognosis.*

- Specify terms that you do not want—*+saturn+ planet not automobile not car not dealer.*

■ Refinements

- Truncate endings (omit *-s, -ed, -ing, -able, -ial, -y/ies* endings). Sometimes you'll give the root word and an asterisk to indicate variations: *corporat** would retrieve documents containing *corporate, corporation, corporations.*

- Omit other connectors, such as *with, of, between.*

- Some search programs allow you to specify a date: *1995–2000* means "1995 through 2000"; *1995, 2000* means "1995 and 2000."

- Some searchers use symbols as connectors:

      and (+ or &)   not (- or !)   or (|)   near (^)

Note: + may mean "must appear."

These symbols are all uppercase of the numerals on the top row of the keyboard; place the symbol immediately before the word you are designating, without spaces. However, check the helpline before using these symbols to find out which to use.

Some programs will allow you to use a long string of phrases linked by punctuation; others may have a limit. You will usually need to do several searches with different keywords, changing your terms so that you get more and more specific information.

Some searchers also allow you to specify the *proximity* of two terms. You might find that it's useful to say that two terms should be mentioned within 10 words of each other (such as *copper* and *patina*), or that you don't want two terms within 10 words of each other (such as *copper* and *mining*). The search engine's instructions will tell you how to write that command.

■ PERIODICALLY, CHECK THE RESULTS

As you research, you will need to make sure that you are getting what you need for your report.

- List the topics for which you have found information.

- Arrange the topics into an outline.

- Note where you still need more information.

- Develop search terms for those missing topics.

- Save the outline on disk to retrieve when you're ready to plan your report.

For example, suppose you found plenty of information on diabetes and then organized the subtopics of that information into this rough outline:

     I. Diabetes: definition
    II. Types of diabetes
   III. Treatment
       A. Insulin
       B. Diet

You would then immediately see that you need information on the role of exercise, since you have already learned that the amount of exercise affects the need for insulin.

Recognizing that gap, you could search again, using "exercise" and related terms.

Use Search Engines and Metasearchers

Do not rely on only one search engine.

Although search engines only find a small percentage of the information that is posted on the Web, often that small percentage is sufficient because of the links those websites in turn provide.

The number of websites on the Internet has doubled in the last year alone. It is not realistic to expect that search engines have been able to keep up with that increase in volume, and they haven't. An article in *Nature* (July 5, 1999) reported that the two most efficient search engines (NorthernLight <http://www.northernlight.com> and Fast Search <http://www.fastsearch.com>—each only found 16 percent of the keywords in posted articles.

However, you need not be daunted by this fact. The nature of the Internet is such that a large number of websites provide links to others, and they in turn provide further links and so on. You just need to plunge in and bookmark the interesting sites as you discover them.

■ Use a Variety of Search Engines

Most people get in the habit of starting with the same search engine for every query, often using the default search engine from their Internet service provider. However, certain search engines are better for particular topics. See the appendix of this book for descriptions and addresses.

In general, use a variety of search engines for even the smallest research project. Note the terms that are repeated in the most relevant articles and use them to refine your search; then use the new search terms with each search engine.

■ Use Metasearchers

Metasearchers search a number of search engines simultaneously. There are several advantages to using them.

- The search is faster because you don't have to type in or click on each search engine's address.

- Metasearchers rephrase your search terms to conform to the rules of each specific search engine.

- Some metasearchers—SavvySearch <http://savvysearch.com> and Highway61 <http://highway61.com>, for example—collate the results by relevancy into a single list. But all metasearchers return just the top 10 or 20 results first, so you won't be overwhelmed with a huge number of responses.

The same query will bring up different results from different search engines, so from the metasearcher's results you may find that one search engine is better for your topic—and for refining your search. Note which search engines find the best websites for your topic, then go to those engines directly for further queries.

For example, entering an inquiry "stress workload workplace" to the metasearcher SavvySearch yielded 30 articles from the search engines All the

Web, Thunderstone, Infoseek, WebCrawler, and HotBot, arranged with the most relevant articles first. Clicking on "search more engines" yielded 30 more articles from AltaVista, Excite, Google, and Lycos. The same inquiry to the metasearcher Dogpile <http://www.dogpile.com> yielded some different articles from AltaVista as well as over 800 articles in Yahoo. The Infoseek articles returned from Dogpile also provided a link to "similar pages," yielding a great list of resources on the subtopic "burnout." See the appendix in this book for more metasearcher addresses.

■ Use FastSearch and NorthernLight.com

Metasearchers are often the fastest source of information, but they don't include the currently most comprehensive search engines —Fast Search <http://www.alltheweb.com> and NorthernLight <http://www.northernlight.com>. Both these search engines are very fast and both avoid the duplication that you find with other search engines. Both allow you to enter multiple terms— in a straight list (without commas or *ands*), the more the better. NorthernLight also allows you to organize the results into folders and to categorize subsequent searches. NorthernLight's private database includes articles available only for a fee, but with the author, title, and date, you may be able to find many of the articles at your library or even on the Internet.

For example, NorthernLight found 275 articles on stress, workload, workplace—many of them different from those found by the metasearchers. One of those articles available for a fee was in *U.S. News and World Report.* Using the date of the article at <http://www.usnews.com>, you could read that article for free.

So the searches with two metasearchers and NorthernLight quickly produced a wealth of information to be analyzed and organized.

Before using your favorite search engine, try these:

FastSearch   <http://www.alltheweb.com>

NorthernLight   <http://www.northernlight.com>

Dogpile   <http://www.dogpile.com>

Highway61   <http://www.highway61.com>

SavvySearch   <http://www.savvy.com>

USE INDEXES
AND OTHER DATABASES

The backbone of many research projects is the information found in scholarly articles.

Databases are electronic storehouses of information. Bibliographic databases (lists of titles of books and articles) are the most common type. These indexes and catalogs will usually give you a brief description or the abstract of a book or article, along with the title, author, publisher, date of publication, and number of pages. Note that some bibliographic databases are on the Web as well. See the appendix of this book for their addresses.

In libraries, some databases are installed in designated computers, but most are listed in a menu on the library's homepage. Look for:

- *Magazine Index* or *Reader's Guide Abstracts*— newspaper and popular magazine articles

- *WestLaw*—law articles

- *Medline*—medical articles

- *ABI/INFORM*—business articles

- *ERIC*—articles on educational issues

Check with the reference desk at your library for information on specialized databases available for your particular topic.

Indexes list the contents for each issue of specified periodicals. Articles *within* magazines, journals, and newspapers are listed in indexes according to author, title, or subject. In addition, some databases give abstracts of the articles and some also give you the text itself to read on the screen or to print out. After finding the titles of articles you want to read, you'll then have to find them in the library. If you are searching your library's collection, the database will often tell you the location of the book or article—whether it's in the reference section, in the stacks, on reverse, on microfilm, or on microfiche.

Citation indexes are lists that include the articles on a particular subject plus information about the references to that article (citations) by other scholars. This cross-referencing can lead you to many other sources, as well as help you select which would be the most important to read. A citation index allows you to find out what experts consider the classics in their field. Be sure to read an expert who is cited often. Citation indexes are organized by discipline. Look in your library for the *Humanities Citation Index*, the *Science Citation Index*, and the *Social Sciences Index.*

Full-text databases are indexes that include the whole text, not just the title. Understandably, there are not as many of these. Most of these full-text databases provide unformatted texts (just straight typing), but others are organized with headings and links to related articles. If you want, you can read entire articles—even books—on the screen or print out the sections you want. On the Internet, some full-text databases require a fee for you to see the actual text. However, selected recent articles are available free from many magazines and most national newspapers. See the appendix of this book for the addresses.

Statistical sources are the fastest way to find statistical information—such as Census Bureau data in the *Population and Housing Counts,* or *The County and City Databook,* or *USA Counties*. If your library subscribes, U.S. government data is collated at <http://www.usgovsearch.com>, or you can go to individual websites of particular agencies. Nonprofit organizations also provide valuable statistics and other information through their websites. See the appendix of this book for some suggestions.

Directories include information of the sort found in phone books. For example, Yahoo! has a particularly good directory for people and businesses. The specialized directories also sort the information by categories, giving you leads to further research. For example, you can see lists of businesses by type, giving corporate officers and annual sales figures. Check your library for *Dun's Business Locator, Dun's Small Business Sourcing File,* and *Standard and Poor's Corporations.*

Some databases have restricted access (you must have a library account, or you must pay a fee). To use such a database, you may need an authorization number and password when using your personal computer.

Three Full-Text Databases to Try

FirstSearch, an excellent resource, includes access to a large number of databases in specific fields of study. It is on the Web for a fee and available free in many libraries.

Click on the subject area and then on the database you wish. Type your specific topic in the search box , click on "Search," and that will retrieve the titles of relevant articles. As you read their descriptions, click on the "tag record box" for those articles you want to read. When you have selected a number of articles, click on "save tags" and then "show all tags." After you review this list, you can then either save the information on the articles to your disk or e-mail them to yourself to use in your bibliography.

Lexis-Nexis, available by subscription, indexes thousands of news articles, including press releases and newswire articles. Although it is expensive, many organizations and public libraries are now allowing at least limited access to this service. It is definitely worth a wait in line. Use the helpline to learn how to use their very sophisticated search tools. To pay for individual searches, go to the website at <http://www.lexis.com>.

CARL (Colorado Alliance of Research Libraries) is a service that lists scholarly articles according to subject. You can order copies of the articles for a fee or you can record the bibliographic information and find the article in your own library. To reach CARL, type in <http://www.uncweb.carl.org/>.

USE LIBRARY CATALOGS, BOOKSELLERS, AND E-TEXTS

The Internet provides a shortcut to the books you'll need for your report.

Although computers have revolutionized the way libraries work, the basic method remains the same as it was in the old print-based days: Librarians catalog books, magazines, newspapers, photographs, and recordings by author, title, and subject, with cross-references to important subtopics within the subject. This information is stored in the library's **catalog,** so you can look for a work by subject—or by author or title if you have that information.

Now that catalogs are electronic, you can search several libraries within the same system simultaneously, and you can search the catalogs of many of the world's libraries from the comfort of your home. As more out-of-print books are available online, you can also read the book or print out selections of it at your computer. See the appendix of this book for some addresses for libraries and online texts.

Books take time to make it into print: Even when an author rushes a manuscript to the publisher, there are editors, reviewers, fact checkers, proofreaders, and the author, once again, to evaluate and correct the manuscript before it gets to the reading public. Those intervening interactions with the content and style of the book add to the quality of what is printed, but of course they also make for delay. Once you have a book in your hand, the information may be thoroughly verified but also surpassed by later events.

Nevertheless, you will probably need to use some books— at least for background or overview. For some topics, books may be the major resource. Whatever your topic, the solid foundation of information that books provide is an important anchor for information from more recent articles— either in journals or on the Internet.

You can find books on your subject by going to your local library's catalog on designated computers, or by looking at online library catalogs, or by checking commercial bookstores online.

■ Search for Subject First

Searches in catalogs can be conducted for author, title, or subject. You may have a particular author or title in mind, but more often, you will be searching for any books available on your subject. When specifying a subject search, enter the keywords. Use alternate terms and Boolean operators (see page 16). Most catalogs allow you to get a "full display," which will give you all the publishing information as well as a brief description of the book, the other subjects it covers, the call number, and whether the book is available.

■ Use Online Library Catalogs

Even when you plan to go to your library, you are usually better off searching first from home if you have home access to the catalog. This way you can print out a list of books, plan your library search, and avoid waiting to use the library's computers. If you use other libraries' catalogs, you'll also have a sense of what information is available and can request an interlibrary loan for a book your own library does not hold.

Research libraries such as the Library of Congress and the New York Public Library have websites that you can consult, giving you the opportunity to look at major listings of books and, in some cases, databases as well. Use a search engine to find a specific library, or check the comprehensive list at <http://sunsite.berkeley.edu/Libweb/usa-acad.html>.

■ Ask a Librarian

Don't be shy; librarians are professional researchers who are there to help you find information. If you don't understand Library of Congress subject headings (the terms indexers use for categorizing books and articles), request help with that list. Ask about your library's special collections or resources on your topic. Most libraries also keep "vertical files" with a variety of resources on the most popular topics. These files will be listed in the library catalog, as will items in the media collections, on computer disk, and on CD-ROM. Ask for help also if you need to read an article on microfilm or microfiche.

■ Use Online Bookstores

There are several reasons for going to the commercial booksellers, such as <http://www.amazon.com>, <http://www.barnesandnoble.com>, <http://www.booksonline.com>, and so forth:

• The latest books may not yet be available in libraries.

- The search is easy to do, and it's free.

- You can get ideas about books on related topics.

- You can get the bibliographical information for a book if you forgot to write it down when you were in the library.

■ USE E-TEXTS

Books in the common domain (that is, those with expired copyrights—usually 75 years after the date of first printing) can be published on the Internet. Some are in just plain typed text, but the Bartleby Project at Columbia University <http://www.columbia.edu/acis/bartleby/index.html> and the Gutenberg Project <http://www.promo.net/pg/> provide attractive texts complete with illustrations. Perhaps you just want to verify a quotation from a scene you remember in Shakespeare's *Midsummer Night's Dream*; consulting the entire play online may be the fastest way to get what you need.

In fact, consulting e-texts may be the only way that you can find documents in their original form. As more historical material is scanned and posted online, that is where you will need to view it—not in the archives of the major research libraries.

In addition, articles in current issues of many journals and newspapers are available online, which may be just what you need if your topic is in this week's news.

See the appendix of this book for other e-text addresses.

CHECK DISCUSSION GROUPS

You can use comments from discussion groups in your report if you take time to verify the information.

The Internet began as a communication network among experts; the best of discussion groups continue that tradition. Amazingly, many individuals continue to volunteer their expertise in answering people's questions.

You may not have time for participating in discussion groups on your topic. However, you can see what others have posted in an asynchronous (not live) group devoted to the particular topic that you are researching. Your job, of course, is to make certain that what is presented is worth citing.

Verify what you find by an alternate route. Check a statistic or an alleged fact in another source. See the chapter entitled "Verify the Information" in Part 2.

Follow a thread so you see what others say in response. The best way to follow public discussion groups is to go to a search engine such as AltaVista <http://www.altavista.com> that tracks the conversation for each topic, regardless of what group is discussing it. AltaVista has indexed, according to topic, the public conversations on Internet message boards and newsgroups. You can follow threads of discussion in an organized way rather than going to the group's posting. You'll find a wide range of quality, from self-indulgent comments to expert opinion. See whether references and alternate points of view are mentioned. Then verify the quality of that information by going to other websites or library sources.

Notice that some ideas can be valuable even when the writer isn't an acknowledged authority. Sometimes an idea just makes sense. See whether you can determine whether the idea is good— perhaps by querying an expert on your own via e-mail or interview. Or just present the comment in your report as an idea submitted in a discussion that makes sense to you.

■ Mailing Lists (Listserv)

If you have a long-term research project, you may decide to subscribe to a mailing list where you can get all the group's messages sent to your e-mail address.

There are organized mailing lists on almost any topic. Some are private e-mail conferences—open only to individuals presenting the necessary credentials; others are available to the public. You can join a public mailing list by sending a message to the organizer. Warning: You will get a flood of e-mail, so select your list carefully. Also be very careful before participating yourself in the conversation; some mailing lists are really professional symposiums, and questions from novices are not welcomed.

Select a list. You can search a list of descriptions and addresses. See page 180. Also read the guidelines for discussion groups beginning on page 37.

There are two types of discussion groups: moderated (where a person or committee selects which messages will be posted to the group) and unmoderated (where the computer sends all messages out to the group, regardless of content). Some groups also sort messages by content (threads), so you can read only those messages that interest you.

Many lists are available through Internet service providers. If your e-mail program doesn't subscribe for you automatically, you'll need to print out and save the directions to subscribe and (most importantly) to unsubscribe.

Listserv is the program that manages the subscription to mailing lists. Note that there are always two addresses—one to subscribe or unsubscribe (the address with *serv* in it), and one to address messages to the group (usually the name of the *group@its address*). Don't confuse the two. Because computers dumbly process your e-mail message, it's equally useless to tell the whole group of subscribers to unsubscribe you as it is to give your remarks on an important topic to the computer that is composing the subscription list.

Submit a request to subscribe by sending an e-mail message according to the directions: Usually, you leave the subject line blank. In the body, you give your real name and e-mail address and add the line "subscribe".

If you can, specify a summary or digest form. (The directions will tell you if that is possible. Often you specify that after you are a subscriber.) The digest form means that you'll get summaries of the messages—an advantage when there are many responses each day, as there sometimes are.

Unsubscribe when you are no longer interested. When you're finished with your project, be sure to unsubscribe, sending the appropriate message as given in the initial directions—usually the same message as your first one with the substitution of the word "unsubscribe" for the word "subscribe," sent to the subscription address.

■ GENERAL ADVICE FOR PARTICIPATING IN DISCUSSION GROUPS ON THE INTERNET

Mailing lists can provide valuable information, as can the previous postings of some discussion groups. However, finding information this way is often less efficient than using subject directories, search engines, and libraries. Plan to join in chats only if you have lots of time to spare.

Read the rules. Every group has guidelines for conversations and routines for sending/responding to messages.

Identify the group's purpose. Some chat rooms, MUDs, and MOOs are just fun places for role-playing, self-expression, and flirting. You probably won't get much material for a research report.

Consult past messages. You may get answers to your questions by reviewing the FAQs (Frequently Asked Questions) or the *archives* (previous messages or postings sent), available through Remarq <http://www.remarq.com> or listed when you subscribe. Be sure to read both for a few days before sending an e-mail query to a mailing list or discussion group yourself. You'll invite negative responses if you ask a question that is redundant or inappropriate. Since some mailing lists are really scholarly conferences by e-mail, check carefully before attempting to participate.

Compose good subject lines. As you scroll through a list of messages in a newsgroup, you'll notice the importance of accurate wording for the subject line. A well-phrased subject line ensures that the message will be read by people who are interested in that topic. Many people ignore messages with vague or emotional subject lines (such as "I need help!"). Give a concise indication of your message: "Request anecdotes on distance learning."

For asynchronous discussions, spend time on composing. Use short paragraphs and revise to eliminate repetition. Proofread and check punctuation.

Quote briefly when replying. You will also notice that some people repeat the entire message they're responding to, since most e-mail programs make it easy to do so. It's preferable to quote briefly from the message you're responding to, using angle brackets on each line to indicate the quote (>) . Some e-mail programs do this automatically. In addition, avoid sending nonsubstantial messages such as "I agree." Reply only when you can contribute to the conversation.

For synchronous conversations, read your message before sending. The fun of synchronous groups comes in part from the speed of the conversation, and it's easy to get caught up in the spirit of the group. Most groups will forgive an occasional typo, but guard against confusing or offending others with a carelessly written message. Whether you are participating in a moderated group or not, if others complain about you, you can be identified and barred permanently from that or related groups if you have violated the rules.

Be wary of getting so caught up in the group that you lose your perspective. Often a relationship that develops online makes you trust the other's opinions. Don't confuse that reaction with researching experts' opinions.

QUERY BY E-MAIL

Often, the fastest way to find information on the Internet is to ask a person.

You may already have enough information to sift through, but often a direct question to an individual can be the most efficient route to getting a good perspective on your topic. Query by e-mail is sent to three distinct audiences:

- People you know—friends, relatives, or other professionals who may be knowledgeable in your field of study.

- People who are paid or who have volunteered to answer inquiries. For example, many businesses and organizations have a button on their homepage where you can click to send e-mail to their office. There are also a number of "ask the experts" websites, some run by universities. See the appendix for some addresses.

- People who haven't volunteered, but may respond anyway.

To discover Internet addresses for the names of people you have encountered whom you'd like to query, consult one of the Internet directories (see page 182). Of course, many individuals don't answer "cold call" queries even from people they know, but a respectful, carefully phrased question might yield a response.

If you do send an e-mail, keep in the mind that your question should be clear, easy-to-read, and, above all, brief. Many people don't mind helping if they can do so quickly. Whether you know the person or not, follow these guidelines to make it easy for the person to respond.

Write a short subject line that is to the point. In their list of incoming messages most e-mail programs give only the first few words of a subject line, so you need to engage the expert's attention quickly.

> Subject line: Tailless salamander

Write a reference line at the top of the body of the message. Your request must be clearly worded; explain exactly what it is you want to know.

> Re: Six tailless salamanders were sighted this weekend in Kirbyville, Texas; do salamanders normally lose their tails this time of year?

Be realistic about what you request. Allow at least a week for response time and ask a question that can be answered quickly.

Explain what you will do with the information. In one or at most two brief paragraphs, indicate your purpose—especially if a public forum is involved.

> I write for the Austin Community College student newspaper and would like to cite your answer in a short article tentatively entitled "Eyes on Nature's World"–about carefully observing nature while hiking.

Promise to give the expert credit. Offer to send a copy of the report. At the bottom of your message, list the expert's full name and professional affiliation; request any corrections so you can be both complete and accurate.

> If you can respond by October 25, I would appreciate it. When you do, please confirm that I have the correct spelling and other details as listed below.

Proofread carefully and spellcheck the message. You cannot expect an answer to a sloppily presented query.

Don't expect too much. Some people may answer past your deadline—or never; others may reply with form messages that don't get to the heart of your question. And of course, no one is going to do all your research for you. Although the quality of answers to e-mail queries can vary widely, it is nevertheless worthwhile to ask.

Check Gopher
and Telnet

Web-based programs have mostly replaced the
older systems for retrieving information.
However, you may still need to use them.

■ Gopher

Gopher is a simple, nongraphic searcher that gives
you a list of choices from which to select and
connects you to research facilities appropriate to
the subject you specify. The name is a tribute both
to the gopher mascot at the University of
Minnesota, where the system was developed, and
to the speed of its retrieval ("go-for").

Although most gopher sites have not been updated
in several years, gopher remains a fast way to
reach some research libraries and a favorite among
users of a slow modem. The best way to find
gopher addresses is via Galaxy <http://www.
einet.net>.

■ Telnet

Even though Telnet can be difficult to use, some
very good libraries and discussion groups are
available only through Telnet. Your library,
computer lab, or Internet service provider should
provide this service with detailed written
instructions. If not, ask a librarian or technical staff
member for help. From home, you can use Telnet
only if you have the necessary software installed.

You will need the Telnet address. You usually encounter one when you're on a website, but check <http://www.einet.net> for a directory. In addition, you will need to write down the logon (letters and numbers that you type in to start the program). Notice that often these are capital letters.

When you use Telnet, what you are doing is communicating with a computer at the distant location. Print or write down the directions before beginning your session.

Allow for lag time before what you have typed appears on your screen. What is happening is that your keyboard is communicating with the distant computer, telling it what you want.

Use arrow keys, not the mouse. Not only is the mouse useless, touching it can sometimes even break the connection.

Enter only the word or number for your choice at the prompt line. Often you give the number of your selection, but sometimes there is a brief code. Other keystrokes may produce very different responses from what you expect. (For example, a mistake may freeze the screen or add an unremovable symbol.)

Always press *enter* **after typing your selection.**

Be sure to sign off properly. The directions at the beginning will give you the sequence of letters or numbers to use to exit the program. If you forget, try pressing *Q* and then *enter*.

Refine Your Search

You will need to do several search sessions for best results. In the time between sessions, evaluate what you have found and modify the next search.

■ Use Different Search Terms

Review the terms you have already used, and look at the results.

- Check a dictionary or thesaurus for alternate wordings, synonyms, and antonyms. Try alternate spellings ("labour or labor," "genealogy or geneology"). If you have been using "horse" in all your searches, adding "equine" and "thoroughbred" will call up different articles. If you are researching part-time and temporary employment, see what information you get with "full-time."

- Use the terms in the articles you've found. For example, you may have found "campylobacter" in an article on food poisoning. Checking for it alone brings up a number of specialized articles.

- Use the names of authors or experts in subsequent searches. For instance, you could list the names referred to in articles on the topic of "deaf culture." Pursuing searches for each of those names in turn could lead you to a website for the teaching of reading to a deaf child, which may be a topic appropriate for the rest of your search.

- Try using fewer words in your query. Sometimes a sophisticated search string bypasses valuable articles.

Try metasearchers again with the refined search terms. If you began your search several weeks earlier, new material may now be available. When using individual search engines, check the rules for advanced searches.

Some search engines will get both "cat" and "cats," whether you enter one or the other word, but others will only get whichever one you specify. Check the helpline or give both words.

■ Stay Open to New Ideas and Interpretations

Your research may lead you to drastically narrow or modify your original topic. You may have begun your research thinking that you would be able to find enough information to discuss, for example, the problems of food poisoning and then found it was much more interesting to look at the government regulation of the food industry regarding sanitation. Your earlier searches on the topic of food poisoning can provide background when you write the report. Subsequent searches will use different search terms, such as "USDA inspectors." In addition, you would need to look at congressional bills at the Thomas site <http://thomas.loc.gov>; at the websites of watchdog groups, such as the Public Interest Research Group <http://www.pirg.org>; and at sites for consumer groups, such as *Consumer Reports* <http://www.consumerreports.org>. Furthermore, discussion groups can steer you into some interesting directions for research. See the appendix of this book for some suggestions about these and other helpful sites.

Try approaching your topic from a different angle. If you've been looking for the processes for eradicating moss, look at what gardeners do to *encourage* moss growth. If you have been looking at health insurance in the United States, look at how other countries provide health care. The details from a different perspective may not go into your report, but considering the opposite point of view will help you make the report more objective in tone.

PART 2

HOW TO ASSESS THE INFORMATION YOU HAVE FOUND

Evaluate Your Sources of Information
Verify the Information
Outline Your Information
Correct Gaps and Overlaps in Information

EVALUATE YOUR SOURCES OF INFORMATION

Even when you get information from a reliable source such as a government document or a respected publication, ask yourself how that information was obtained and how it can be verified. Use this chapter as a checklist to evaluate Internet sources.

■ BE SKEPTICAL

Errors can occur. The most prominent experts can make mistakes. Typos and editing errors happen—especially with computerized corrections—even in prestigious publications. If a particular statistic seems off-base, see whether you can corroborate it in another source.

Appearances can be deceiving. It's easy to create a professional-looking website. Even grade-schoolers can now do so if they have the proper software and a little training, so don't be fooled by a sharp image. However, don't be put off by resources using plain text (just straight typing). Many government, educational, and nonprofit sites post valuable reports but do not have the budget to hire technicians who could design the site for visual interest and hyperlinks.

Anyone can claim to be an authority. In particular, don't rely on information you get from discussion groups; always find another source for verification.

Human beings have biases. Even a person who is trying hard to be fair may not understand another perspective, or may be motivated by a particular political or personal agenda.

The popularity of a particular view doesn't make it correct. The speed with which data is transmitted on the Internet makes its material particularly vulnerable. Notice how quickly jokes and rumors spread, and also be aware that the number of "hits" (visitors) to a site may be the result of a number of marketing ploys, promising something the site doesn't deliver.

Be very suspicious if you find these characteristics on a website:

- No author or organization listed on the page

- No date of last revision

- Typographical errors

■ Evaluate the Quality of the Material

The last three digits designate the type of institution at the Internet address. Just as there is a difference between scholarly journals and magazines for the general public, there is a difference between a document on a commercial website and an article posted by an educational, governmental, or nonprofit site. Often the address is a clue to the purpose of the document.

There is obviously a hierarchy of quality to articles you can find electronically. Some very good information is published (in the spirit of the Internet) outside the conventional review and editing process. However, some individuals can sound very authoritative when they really don't understand the complexities of the subject.

Distinguish between primary and secondary sources. Primary sources are produced by someone involved with the subject you are studying. For example, for a research project on the film director Martin Scorsese, primary sources include his films and publications as well as interviews with him. Secondary sources are produced by people who have studied the subject. For a study of Scorsese, secondary sources would include film reviews, biographies, and histories—as well as interviews with actors and film technicians he has worked with.

Identify the intended audience. Often the first few lines will tell you whom that website is addressing. For example, the primary audience may be children, people committed to a particular agenda, the general public, or scholars. Once you've identified the intended audience of the website, you will be able to sift out the information that is not appropriate for a college report.

Identify the purpose. A commercial website (one whose address ends in .com) is often selling a product; a nonprofit (.org) site may have a political, religious, or social agenda. An article at an educational (.edu) site may have been written by a student in a class rather than by a professor.

Check the author and affiliated organization. You may have come across an author before in your research, making it easier to evaluate the level of expertise. But what if you can't tell whether the author has published on this topic before or is affiliated with a professional organization or institution? Try doing a search just for the author's name—either with a search engine or with one of the directories listed in the appendix of this book.

When you encounter a webpage and there is no date, author, or institution given, look at the Internet address. Try reaching the main page by deleting all the extensions (letters and numbers after slashes or periods) after what is the main address (which would end, for example, in .edu or .org or .gov). The main page should tell you the affiliation and date of original posting or latest revision; the links should identify the author, department, or agency. Find out the reputation of a sponsoring organization or affiliation by plugging its name into a search engine.

Look for signs of high quality. Footnotes and lists of references demonstrate careful research. Links to other high-quality sites (and links by others to this particular site) show that the site is "in the loop" of reputable information providers.

Try to find out whether the document was published under professional review. Professional publications (with editors, fact checkers, and review panels) stand behind the quality of their articles. And now, those articles are often published on the Web. But an article can look just as professional (even more attractive) and not be authoritative. Look for references to an affiliated organization or to previous publication in a respected journal. Very often, this information appears at the end of the document. Sometimes you will only see a logo (symbol with some initials). If so, go to a search engine and see what you can find for those initials.

Note the date of latest revision. Your topic will determine how recent your information must be. Most sites should be updated at least monthly, but some information is obsolete within a few hours. On the other hand, material for historical topics should not be updated except to make corrections; a scholarly paper on Zora Neale Hurston will probably be an important resource, even though it was posted six years ago.

Examine the coverage of the topic. In-depth analysis requires length. What subtopics are covered? Does the coverage appear to be balanced with opposite points of view presented? Does the article refer to evidence to support the various points made? Are there citations or links to other sources?

Is the article well written? Many scholars are not stylists, to be sure, but the material should be well organized, with no more than an occasional typo or error in punctuation. Look at the overall tone of the presentation; it should be objective, with the implied intention to inform.

Verify the
Information

Use statistical sources and focused search
engines to get the facts you will need for your
report.

**Find an independent verification for most
information.** Use the journalists' guidelines and
find an independent source to verify your major
information. Obviously, you don't need two
sources for population figures; the U.S. Census
Bureau's statistics (although contested) are used in
the United States as a matter of law. But you
should always try to find another source for any
material presented as fact in discussion groups and
on individuals' homepages.

Sometimes it's as simple as checking another
website, but at other times you may have to
interpret information by examining the larger
picture. For example, the rate of divorce in the
United States is currently on the decline. What
does this mean? At first glance, you might think
that the number of stable marriages must therefore
be rising. However, that is not the case. Instead,
there are fewer Americans marrying in the first
place, and when they do marry, it is at a later age.
You can get these statistics from the Census Bureau
at <http://www.fedstats.gov>.

**Be particularly careful about getting all your data
from a single report.** You should do so no matter
how reliable it may appear to be. Not only might
the author have selected only those statistics that
support a particular point of view, but there may

be errors in the document itself. Letters and numbers may get transposed, and spellcheckers won't catch an inaccurate number or correctly spelled wrong word. Corrections are often published well after the original dateline. It is worth checking the next few issues of a journal or newspaper publishing a substantial report, just to see whether there were any corrections.

For example, in researching urban sprawl you may have come across an article in the *New York Times* (July 14, 1999) saying that for every 10 percent increase in road size there has been a 5 percent increase in travel time. How can you verify that statistic?

Consult federal agencies. The United States Bureau of Transportation posts all sorts of studies of highways, road use, travel time, and driving behavior. You can find the results fastest by going to <http://www.fedstats.gov> or for a fee to <http://www.usgovsearch.com>, or you can use a search engine, entering the query *highway "travel time" increase.* Any of these searches will take you to the Bureau of Transportation studies at <http://www.bts.gov>.

Consult a site that allows you to ask questions. A number of sites allow you to ask a question and then link you to sites that may have the answer. See the appendix of this book for the addresses.

Ask a person. Who would be most likely to know? Regarding the statistic on highway travel time, it would be the reporter who wrote the article or the authors of the studies cited. It's a long shot, but you might try e-mailing the author in care of the *New York Times.* Since one of the studies mentioned was completed in England, you might also try using a search engine for the phrase *highway and "travel time,"* specifying a site in the United Kingdom.

Use reference resources. At the Librarians' Index to the Web <http://www.lii.org/InternetIndex> as well as on the homepages of most search engines are statistical sources, databases, encyclopedias, and atlases with the results of surveys, studies, charts of demographics, and so forth. See also the appendix of this book for other key resources.

Outline Your
Information

Review what you have discovered and assess
your progress towards the report.

**List the categories for the information you have
accumulated.** Go through your notes and do one of
the following:

- List the categories of information each source
  has covered.

- List the categories you have found and which
  sources cover them.

- Imagine a paper based on the notes you have
  and then list the topics your notes can support
  in such a paper.

Arrange the categories into a simple outline
(or a topic "tree" with subtopic "branches").
At this point, you should be listing only the
categories of information you have *found* with
topics and subtopics, not the places where you
found the information, or categories you wanted
to find.

Identify where you need more information. You
should immediately see where the holes are—
either where evidence is needed to support a point
or where further explanation is needed.

Identify information that doesn't fit. You won't be
able to find a place for everything you have
discovered.

For example, suppose that you got a lot of information on corporate spying, and these were the categories you identified:

> Profiles of corporate spies (examples)
> Foreign capture of U.S. trade secrets (examples)
> FBI investigations
> Description of U.S. law
> Definition of legal corporate spying
> Surveys of companies–trends
> Means of spying–insider, outsider, electronic, telephone
> Descriptions of security precautions

These topics could be organized into a good problem-solution paper, perhaps with this outline:

I. Definition of intellectual property (summary of the law)
II. Corporate spying–legal
   A. "Competitive intelligence" (definition)
   B. Examples
III. Corporate spying–illegal
   A. Means
      1. Insider
      2. Outsider
      3. Electronic
      4. Telephone taps
   B. Regulations
IV. General problems for business
   A. Foreign examples and FBI investigations
   B. Trends and financial examples
V. Solutions
   A. Security
   B. Employee training

You could then mark on your outline where your examples and notes from your research would fit as well as where you need to get more information.

Reminder: Don't discard information that doesn't work for you at this stage; you can't predict what the next research session may find. You may discover some new material that helps you see what you have from a different perspective.

Correct Gaps and Overlaps in Information

Look at your outline for any places where you need facts, for any gaps in the reasoning, or for any confusing or contradictory overlaps. These spots will tell you where you need to do more research.

It often happens that searches produce uneven results—lots of information in one area and nothing in another aspect of your topic. Your interests will dictate what you do at this point. Here are some possible next steps:

Eliminate some subtopics. Let's say that you have lots of stories about what corporate spies did. You might decide to expand your discussion of the methods of corporate spying and then to refer only briefly in your conclusion to the preventive methods. On the other hand, you might prefer to discuss the mechanics of prevention and analyze the process of control. Depending on what you already have, you could then determine whether further research would be necessary.

Get more facts. You may have plenty of opinions and commentary but need some dates or statistics. See the appendix of this book for some addresses for encyclopedias, statistical sources, or experts to query.

Follow up on the names of experts. You might want to get more information on the professional expertise of some of the authorities you cite to give added weight to their remarks.

Get a third opinion. If two of your sources contradict one another, you'll need to find someone who can resolve the discrepancy. When two sources overlap, you can choose the better phrasing for quotations, paraphrase them both, or find out whose credentials are better respected.

Modify your topic. There are two reasons for changing your topic: your interests were engaged by one area of the research, or you didn't find what you expected.

For example, you might have begun your search on corporate spying and then gotten interested in the subtopic of the privacy of e-mail and voice mail. Developing the topic of privacy in the work world would probably take you to sites discussing the use of employer-provided equipment, reports of lawsuits against employers who inspected employees' private messages, how corporate files are maintained, and so forth. With privacy as your main topic, you would need to write a different outline from the one in the previous chapter, but you could probably include some of the information you have already gathered.

On the other hand, you could have been really excited about a topic but none of your searches turned up enough data. If you've followed the different avenues to information described in Part 1 with poor results, don't continue the search. Instead, browse again, as discussed in "Find Your Focus" in Part 1. Get tips on time management in "Acknowledge the Time Limits of Your Project" in Part 3 before you go too much further in your research. Then use your modified topic and begin your search again through the various types of resources described in Part 1.

At this point, the amount and quality of the information you have found will determine whether you can start writing the report or whether you need more research sessions.

PART 3

TIPS FOR ORGANIZING YOUR PROJECT

Keep Your Audience in Mind
Determine the Level of Information You
    Need
Plan to Use Printed Sources
Acknowledge the Time Limits of Your
    Project
Record Information as You Research
Know When to Stop Your Search

KEEP YOUR AUDIENCE IN MIND

Before you begin your research project, be clear about how your report will be evaluated.

Whatever your topic, your research should be motivated by a need to learn something new or to see what you already know in a new way. A research assignment that doesn't change you has failed. Research is required in the academic world precisely because it is a way of informing yourself—and others, once your report is formally presented. In the professional world, research can validate a previously held opinion, but it may also point to new directions if you remain open.

■ FOR STUDENT REPORTS

When you will be submitting your report for a grade, the teacher is the primary audience—even when the report will be shared with the class or posted on the Web. Make sure you understand what characteristics the teacher expects the paper to have.

Most teachers evaluate student papers with basic principles of research in mind. Use these goals to guide you as you begin your search for information and later to determine what should go into the report. The report should show that:

- You have found a good variety of sources of information—sources appropriate to the level of the course (neither too lightweight nor too advanced).

- You have understood the sources and their place in your field of study.

- You have verified the information and analyzed the presentations, comparing them to those of others.

- You have followed the format and other conventions specified for reports in your particular discipline. See Part 4 of this book.

Teachers may value some additional aspects—creativity, or precision in format, or references to themes covered in class. You can often tell a teacher's emphasis by the way the assignment is presented, but ask if the goal is not clear. And if you have not been told, find out the minimum page- or word-count and the number of resources (books and articles) expected.

■ For Professional Reports

The reader of a professional report above all needs to be convinced that you know what you are talking about.

- The report should demonstrate a thorough search for and understanding of information—whether it be only in published material (libraries and the Internet) or also in the field itself—in the laboratory, on location, interviewing those with experience, observing or living with the details of the subject itself.

- The report should be organized to feature what is important and to subordinate the supporting details.

- The report should be simultaneously objective and persuasive—so the reader accepts the conclusions or recommendations.

Determine the Level of Information You Need

You won't know how much research is necessary until you look at what you already know, what the audience expects, and what the audience doesn't need to be told.

■ Acknowledge Your Level of Expertise

If you are new to your topic, you can do a quick subject search on the Internet for background and history. Check encyclopedias and other references online. Check reference books and textbooks in your library. After some basic research, you can decide what areas you will concentrate on.

If you already know a great deal about your topic, identify the aspects where you want more information. List the organizations, locations, and experts' names you already know; list the technical terms, including synonyms; then you can frame your questions for research.

■ Identify the Kinds of Sources That You Will Be Studying

To write a report addressed to colleagues, a marine biologist will need to use scientific journals and websites posted by other marine scientists. Although general interest publications (such as *Newsweek* or the *New York Times*) might have reports on the topic, these articles would probably be referred to only obliquely in a specialist's report, if at all. However, the *New York Times* and *Newsweek* websites are great places to begin for research topics for a freshman-level project in almost any general-interest field.

Materials that you use for personal entertainment would not ordinarily be appropriate for a college research paper, but a report on rap music will necessarily include newsletters, websites aimed at music fans, and liner notes from CDs.

■ IDENTIFY THE AMOUNT OF DETAILED INFORMATION THAT YOU WILL NEED

A 20-page paper needs much more detailed information and analysis than a 5-page one. A paper on narcolepsy will be much more complex for an audience of neuroscientists than for English 101.

You may just need a few facts and a couple of expert opinions, or you may need to show that you have done an almost exhaustive review of the resources available. Again the audience, the purpose, and the required length of the report will help you decide. As a guide, you will need to support any generalizations you make, but often a single fact or quotation will suffice—if you have checked to make sure that the generalization is true.

■ Identify What Your Audience Already Knows

Sometimes, your audience is very familiar with the resources you will be studying (and may even have written some of them). In that case, there will be some background information and explanation that would be most inappropriate in the report, even though you may need to do preliminary research to bring yourself up to speed. At other times, the audience may not be knowledgeable about your subject at all and you will need to include some background—even if you already knew it before your research.

When you are in doubt about what the audience knows, you can present background information in a separate section of the report or preceded by a qualifier ("Researchers have identified . . ." or "Most Americans would agree . . .").

Plan to Use Printed Sources

This book emphasizes electronic sources. Some of those sources, however, will only identify the *titles* of articles or books; you will still need to go to the library to read them and take notes. For most projects, some of the information will be available only in print. However, even when a book or article is on the Web, you may prefer to read it in print.

Many electronic texts of articles are devoid of formatting. Often, you get just plain typeface—many screenfuls that you have to search through carefully to find what you want. In contrast, print articles are easy to skim. You can select passages to read in a long article, noting headings, illustrations, featured quotations, and so forth.

You can browse in print, sampling a middle chapter, for example, or flipping through the table of contents, endnotes, or index of a book.

Many versions of older documents are presented out of context. Text-only electronic versions of older printed articles have been removed from the surrounding pages and format of the original. For some topics, you can get a useful sense of history and culture when you view the accompanying graphics, other articles, and advertisements adjacent to the article as it originally appeared in the newspaper or journal.

It's difficult to get a sense of the length of some computerized texts. You can immediately tell the size of a book or article in print. However, you won't necessarily know the length of an electronic document even when the size of the file is given (for example, 15K) because some of those kilobytes may be for graphics or large font size. (Without graphics, 15K in #12 typeface is about six pages.) If the information is given, note the pages an article covered in its original form.

On the other hand, computers can save you a great deal of time. Use computerized indexes and catalogs first wherever possible. Even if you read a source on paper, use a computer for taking notes. Return to the electronic version of any source that is available so you can copy and paste any quotations—as well as the Internet address, author, title, and so forth—right with the notes, so you'll later be able to document it easily and avoid plagiarism.

Acknowledge the Time Limits of Your Project

If the deadline is rapidly approaching, you will need to be very focused as you research.

Plan to spend one-third of the available time on research. Spend the rest on analyzing information and writing the report. With electronic research, you can quickly get a great deal of information. However, researching electronically can become a mesmerizing activity, and you might find that at the end of a pleasant afternoon there is nothing to report. Try setting a timer (some computers have this feature installed), stopping every hour or so to make sure you have something concrete, so you aren't caught empty-handed at the deadline.

Narrow your topic as soon as possible. It's almost impossible to write a good report on a general topic. For example, don't waste valuable time continuing to research "diabetes." Instead, look at treatments for diabetes or progression of the disease. Use additional terms as you come across them in the results from your queries.

Limit your search to accessible materials. Use what is quickly available. For example, you could put together a good report on a famous author such as Virginia Woolf (if you've already read some of her writing) by limiting your research to books and articles on a particular theme in her work that you already understand.

- You could use standard English literature resources such as the *MLA* (Modern Language Association) *Bibliography* on CD-ROM, the *Humanities Index* (also on CD-ROM), and whatever books in your library are available on the subject of Woolf or twentieth-century British authors in general.

- If your library subscribes, you could log on to FirstSearch and look under "Literature."

- On the Internet, AltaVista <http://www.altavista.com> returned 12,425 results on a simple query on "Virginia Woolf." The first result was for the International Virginia Woolf Society <http://www.utoronto.ca/IVWS>, which provides annual bibliographies. You could then get the listed articles you want from your college library. If you still had time, the first few listings by AltaVista included several good academic webpages as well, where you could get ideas to discuss and cite in your paper.

For most reports, those searches should provide enough information. Don't forget that you still must analyze what you have found and then incorporate what you understand from Woolf's writings into the report. When time is a factor, gathering the data should not take up the majority of your time; use your energy for analysis and careful presentation.

Ask for help. If you will be connecting to the Internet from home, don't forget to allow time to use the library where you'll need to consult print sources—and perhaps get a librarian's help. Use helplines for search engines and databases.

Don't outline too soon. Restrain yourself (at least for a couple of research sessions) from outlining or planning the report itself. Instead, first take some time to discover what you didn't know before, and then allow yourself time to see any patterns within the information. Follow the search process and see what you can discover. After that, you can develop an outline that uses the most valuable information and your thoughts about it.

Allow time for reflection while you research. You can't write a thoughtful report if you have no time to think. Pausing occasionally to jot down your ideas as you work will enable you to see both an emerging general picture of your topic and the quality of the specific information. Even under the pressure of a deadline, you can stay open to discovery. A few minutes using a different index or browsing among adjacent texts on the library bookshelf may yield surprising information or a refreshing point of view.

Plan your reading time. You won't need to read every single word in every source you use, but you will need time for analysis and interpretation. Introductions, conclusions, headings or chapter titles, selected paragraphs—all can give you a sense of the main approach of a particular work.

Take breaks. Stop briefly to stretch every 30 minutes to prevent hand and eye strain. Watch your posture at the computer. Plan to get some sleep before revising the report; a fresh view will improve the paper.

RECORD INFORMATION AS YOU RESEARCH

As you research, save your information on disk. Periodically stop to write down your own thoughts.

Have a couple of formatted computer disks, paper, and pen handy for every research session. Once you find valuable information, save it immediately to disk. Make backups frequently. Bookmark each source, and note the Internet address if your browser does not automatically do so.

■ MAINTAIN GOOD COMPUTER FILES

You can highlight and copy information or pictures and then save them on your disk. See page 145 for directions. Keep separate files according to these types:

- Notes on information (data, statistics, biographical or historic facts)—with the source and date retrieved on each one, right next to the information.

- Downloaded information, marked as an exact copy (to prevent plagiarism) and listing the author, title, web address and date retrieved. Later you can take notes or select passages from the material, but keep these files separate from your own notes.

- Lists of categories and search terms as they occur to you—these will help you plan further searches and organize the information you have discovered.

- General thoughts on the topic, reactions to material you have found, and ideas on the report you must write.

This method will ensure that when you are ready to write the report, some of it will already be written, and you will have the necessary information to prevent plagiarism.

■ Use Disks for Backup

Even when doing all your research from your own computer, you should backup on disk or zip drive all your information—including bookmarks—before ending each session. Do not erase original files when you modify them; instead, rename the revision with the original file name plus a sequential letter or number (e.g., *background1*). Sometimes information you have discarded may become relevant after further research. Similarly, computer crashes wipe out your search history, and you will need to revisit some sites as your research progresses.

■ Record the Source of Every Fact or Quotation

When you are ready to take notes, again save them right on your disk, together with the specific information you will need for documentation.

For an article from a database on CD-ROM:
Author (if given). Title of article. Date of article (if

given). Title of database. City of publication: Publisher, date of copyright.

For an article on the Internet: Author or organization. Title of article (or type of article if e-mail or posting to a message board). Title of website. Organization if different from author. Date of last revision or copyright (if given). Date you viewed it and complete Internet address.

For an article that was printed elsewhere but that you got online: Author. Title of article. Title of publication. Date, volume number, and pages (if given). Title of website. Date you viewed it and complete Internet address.

For a book that you got online: Author. Title. City of publication, publisher, and date of publication. Title of website. Date you viewed it and complete Internet address.

KNOW WHEN TO STOP YOUR SEARCH

The problem most researchers encounter is gauging how much time to allow for the search and for the report. One thing you can count on is that writing the report almost always will take much longer than you expect.

Add your thoughts as you assemble the notes from your electronic sources. Since computers allow you to write and research intermittently, add your commentary and interpretation as you are copying and pasting material from your various sources, being clear each time to put quotation marks around exact wording from others. Give the author, title, and date right below the material so most of your documentation is also done. (See Part 4, "How to Document the Information You Use.")

Stop periodically to see whether you have enough information. Compare the length of your notes to the required size of the finished report. You may already have enough information if you have double the required number of sources and have notes close to the page requirement.

Take time to cull out information that doesn't belong in the report. Often an interesting fact or anecdote has no place. Write an outline and then reject what doesn't fit.

Allow time to write your analysis and commentary. The worst kind of research reports just present the information source by source, with little or no thoughtful commentary. You will need to break up the material that you have found, to analyze it, and to contrast the points of view of the different authorities.

Plan for additional research time. You may at the last minute discover gaps in your information or need to check Internet addresses.

PART 4

HOW TO DOCUMENT THE INFORMATION YOU USE

Reporting All the Sources of Your Information

When you write your report, provide the source for every idea, creative work, or fact.

You are legally and morally required to give appropriate credit. The material you find electronically was put there by someone, and—just as you must do for other sources of information—your report must tell who supplied the ideas. On many websites, you will notice a line from the author granting permission to reproduce the material for personal or educational use—but you still have to give that author credit. Aside from being fair, there are several reasons to give credit:

- You need the authority of the source as support for the quality of your research and the legitimacy of your conclusions.

- You will be adding to honest and intelligent discussion of your topic.

- The reader of your paper can consult your sources firsthand if desired.

- You're likely to be discovered if you don't give credit, since your readers have the same Internet access as you.

- The penalty for plagiarism is severe (failure of the course or expulsion from college; professional humiliation in the business world).

Avoid the temptation to reproduce huge chunks of electronic material. It is tempting to keep

passages you have found in their original form—
particularly because everything is already typed!
As you were working, you should have kept clear
records on all material that you copied, with the
appropriate citation information. If you find a
place where you are unsure, revisit the website and
print out the entire section you used so you can
check to avoid plagiarism. If you don't remember
the website, select a few long phrases from that
section in your paper; submit them, in quotation
marks, to several search engines. That's what
anyone checking your research would do. The
search engines should find that unique string of
phrases.

Be sure that your thoughts dominate the report.
Your paper should present your interpretation of
what you have found, supported by the facts and
opinions you cite. In other words, don't just string
your findings together without reacting to the
information: Analyze and interpret the data, in a
logical sequence, according to your sense of the
most important points. Keep quotations to a
minimum. Particularly when you are writing a
report on the graduate or professional level, your
own expertise *must* be clear.

**Give credit for information in the body of your
paper as well as at the end.** Make certain that you
place quotation marks around any phrases taken
from another person's writing or speech, and tell
where you got those phrases. All the
documentation styles require that you indicate
indebtedness to a source in the body of your paper
while you are presenting information. However,
you don't need to clutter the body of your paper
up with Internet addresses. Just give the briefest
reference you can, so that interested readers can
turn to the end of your paper to find the specific
source.

Get permission to publish copyrighted materials.
You may reproduce copyrighted audios, visuals, or graphics in a paper submitted for a class, but if you publish the paper—on the Web or in any public forum—you must get permission. In addition to giving all the information for the source, be sure to add a tag line, "reproduced by permission."

Give enough information that your reader can find your source. Even when material is in the public domain (available to everyone), you must identify both the original author and where you found the information. For electronic sources in particular, give as complete a description as you can.

The precise format for reporting electronic sources has been evolving—parallel to the popularity of the Internet and more particularly that of the World Wide Web for research. When in doubt, use as your guide the format your discipline requires for an article in a scholarly journal.

General Guidelines

Give all the publishing information for materials that first appeared in print. Follow the format required by your discipline, then give the electronic information. Do not give electronic information that directed you to a document that you then read only in print.

Don't mix italics and underlining. MLA and APA styles prefer that titles of larger works be underlined because they are easier to read. However, if you publish electronically you should italicize.

Give the date of your visit when citing electronic sources that can change, such as a website, a regularly updated online resource, or radio and television programs. The copyright date is sufficient for citing electronic sources that don't change, such as films, CDs, computer programs, or databases stored on CD-ROMs.

Give both the posting and the retrieval addresses for discussion groups and mailing lists. The posting address is where the article first appeared; the retrieval address is where the reader of your paper would have to go to read the article.

Break Internet addresses only after a slash. When listing addresses that are too long to fit on one line, give only as much of the address on each line as you can before a slash (/), not after a hyphen. Do not insert a hyphen, spaces, or any other marks. The reader should be able to assume that, without the line breaks, the address is accurate.

If the academic research style you are using allows it, surround with angle brackets (< >) any addresses that occur at the end of a sentence before adding a period. Otherwise, end the sentence with the final character of the address (no period).

Do not separate your sources by type, such as books, articles, e-mail, CD-ROMs, and so forth, unless told to do so.

Follow the formatting requirements for your particular area of study. Consult a writing handbook or your teacher's guidelines for the general format of your report. The discipline within which you are reporting determines the style.

Check the following chapters for your formatting options.

Using the MLA (Modern Language Association) Style

The MLA style is used for courses in English, foreign languages, film, and literature.

◼ Format for Citations in the Body of Your Paper

With the MLA style, you give parenthetical citations after presenting information in the body of the paper. After the fact or quotation, give, in parentheses, the last name of the author of the source plus the page number where the fact or quotation appeared. The source is then listed fully at the end of the paper in the Works Cited.

However, electronic sources may not have numbered pages. If the paragraphs are numbered, give that number preceded by the abbreviation *par.* Otherwise, just give the author's last name. If no author is listed, give the first main word of the title (or the first phrase, if the first word is common to other titles). Without a number for page or paragraph, you will not need a parenthetical citation for your electronic source if you identify the author in your sentence.

> Jason P. Mitchell interprets Maggie and Big Daddy as "less sympathetic" and Brick as "more compelling" (par. 4).

MLA

> The characters in <u>Cat on a Hot Tin Roof</u> can be viewed differently in light of Tennessee Williams's comments in an interview (Mitchell par. 4).

The reader of your paper could then turn to the Works Cited where you have listed the complete reference. (The first date is the date of posting; the second date is the date you viewed it.)

> Mitchell, Jason P. "The Artist as Critic: A Reconsideration of Brick Pollitt." 5 Dec. 1995. 5 June 1999 <http://sunset.backbone.olemiss. edu/%7Ejmitchel/misphil.htm>.

■ FORMAT FOR LISTING SOURCES AT THE END OF YOUR PAPER

Heading: Center the heading, Works Cited. Use caps and lowercase, without underline, boldface, italics, or quotation marks.

Sequence: Make one list, not separated by type of source. Alphabetize by the last names of the authors. When no author is listed, alphabetize by the first main word of the title. Include *a, an,* or *the,* but ignore these words when alphabetizing. **Do not number the list.**

Spacing: Double-space the entire list with no extra space between entries.

Indentation: Start the first line of each entry at the left margin. Indent subsequent lines for that entry five spaces or half an inch. End each entry with a period.

Authors' Names: Reverse authors' names: last name, first name. Give initials or Jr. if listed, but not M.D. or Ph.D. If the author is an organization, give its title without "the."

> Jamiesen, Brendan, Jr.

> National Coalition for the Homeless.

Reverse only the first author's name if there are several. With four or more authors, list the first and then write et al., meaning "and others."

> Brooks, Veronica, and David Ennis.

> Pond, Sarah, et al.

When the same author has written more than one work, give the author's full name only for the work that is first in alphabetical order. Then use three hyphens and a period in place of the author's name as you list each of the other works.

> National Council for the Homeless. Statement on Census 2000 Service Based Enumeration. 28 Mar. 2000 <http://nch.ari.net/census2000.html>.

> ---. Why Are People Homeless? June 1999. 19 Oct. 1999 <http://nch.ari.net/causes.html>.

Titles: Underline titles of main works—books, newspapers, websites, and CD-ROMs. Use

MLA

quotation marks around the titles of shorter works that appear inside the larger ones—such as articles, stories, chapters, and sections. Do not underline the end punctuation marks in titles.

Dates: List day month year with no commas. Abbreviate all months but May, June, and July. List both the date of the original copyright or posting as well as the date you viewed the source, unless you are certain that it is an unchanging source, such as a CD-ROM or video.

Internet Addresses: Surround addresses with angle brackets (< >), with one space before the opening angle bracket and a period after the closing one.

■ GUIDELINES FOR SPECIFIC SOURCES

Standalone Database or CD-ROM

Author (if given). "Title." (or the heading of the material you read) <u>Title</u> and publishing information of original in print, if known. <u>Title of the database.</u> Publication medium. City of publication and vendor (if relevant), electronic publication date.

> Kael, Pauline. "Pauline Kael Review: <u>West Side Story.</u>" <u>I Lost It at the Movies.</u> <u>Cinemania 97.</u> CD-ROM. Redmond, WA: Microsoft, 1996.

MLA

Online Source or Website

Author or organization (if known). "Title of the article (if part of a larger website)." <u>Title of the website.</u> Date of publication or last revision (if given). Date you viewed it <address of the website>.

> North Texas Institute for Educators on the Visual Arts. <u>Pioneer Plaza Cattle Drive by Robert Summers.</u> 28 Oct. 1998. 30 June 1999 <http://www. art.unt.edu/ntieva/artcurr/public/sos/ sos5.htm>.

Original Source in Print, but Viewed on a Website

Author or organization (if known). "Title of the article (if appropriate)," <u>Title of the Complete Work.</u> Publishing information for original print version (if known). <u>Title of the website where you viewed it.</u> Date of original posting. Online publisher. Date of latest revision. Date you viewed it <Internet address>.

> Jewett, Sarah Orne. <u>The Country of the Pointed Firs.</u> Boston: Houghton [c1910]. <u>Project Bartleby.</u> New York: Columbia U Academic Information Systems, July 1996. 4 Aug. 1999 <http://www.columbia. edu.acis/bartleby/jewett/100.html>.

> Kiernan, Vincent. "How Egalitarian Societies Rein in Potential Despots," <u>Chronicle of Higher Education.</u> 17 Dec. 1999. 19 Dec. 1999 <http://www.chronicle. com/weekly/v46/i17/ 17a02201.htm>.

MLA

Lederer, Richard, and Richard Downs.
"Chapter One: Sleeping Dogs and
Other Ponderables," <u>Sleeping Dogs
Don't Lay: Practical Advice for the
Grammatically Challenged.</u> New York:
St. Martin's, 1999. 22 Feb. 2000
<http://www.wnyc.org/musicculture/s
horts/readingindex.html>.

Article from a Newswire, Viewed on a Website

Cooper, Mike. "U.S. Confirms West Nile
Virus Caused N.Y. Deaths." Reuters.
21 Oct. 1999. 26 Oct. 1999 <http://
news.lycos.com/stories/science/199
91021RTSCIENCE-HEALTH->.

Direct E-Mail to You (Not a Discussion Group)

Although MLA does not require it, indicating the
person's title or area of expertise in brackets lends
authority to your citation:

Author [title or area of expertise]. E-mail to the
author (that's you). Date.

Young, Sally [Ph.D, Professor of English,
U of Tennessee]. E-mail to the
author. 2 Apr. 1999.

Posting to a Discussion Group

Real name of author (if known). "The subject line
of the article." Online posting. The date of

MLA

the posting. The group to which it was sent—multiple groups separated by a comma. The date you viewed it <where the article can be retrieved>.

Winkel, Rich. "Media-US: Censored Stories also Win Prizes." Online posting. 14 May 1998. Misc.activism. progressive. 6 June 1999 <http://x12. deja.com/getdoc.xp?AN=3533125 23.1&CONTEXT=897566203.166 199459&hitnum=25>.

A Graphic or Multimedia Image Inserted into Your Paper

Artist or director (if known). The title of the art (if given). The title of the website. The date of the posting. The date you viewed it <where the image was found>.

Barry's Clip Art Server. 13 Dec. 1999 <http://www.barrysclipart.com/anim ations/images/0139.gif>.

An Online Audio or Multimedia Image Discussed in Your Paper

Artist or director (if known). The title of the art (if given). The title of the website. The date of the posting or latest update. The date you viewed it <where the image was found>.

Ryder, Winona. Girl Interrupted (Trailer). Sony Pictures Entertainment (SPE!) Movies. 14 Dec. 1999. 14 Dec. 1999 <http://www.spe.sony.com/ movies/girlinterrupted/assets/girl_tra iler160.mov>.

MLA

A Recorded Audio or Multimedia Image Discussed in Your Paper

If you discussed the entire work, refer to the format in which it is available:

Artist or director. Dir. (for director, if necessary) "Title of Song (if applicable)." <u>Title of album or film.</u> Format. City: Production Company, date.

> Hitchcock, Alfred. Dir. <u>Vertigo.</u> VHS. Universal City: Paramount, 1958. Restored vers. 1996.

> Segovia, Andres. "Segovia: Study (Estudio sin Luz)." <u>A Centenary Celebration, Disc 3.</u> Universal City: Decca, 1994.

A sample Works Cited page follows.

■ SAMPLE WORKS CITED, MLA STYLE

WORKS CITED

"Online Buffs Hit and Miss on Manners." <u>U.S. News Online.</u> 22 Mar. 1999. 3 Dec. 1999 <http://www.usnews.com/usnews/issue/990322/22beha.htm>.

Pearce, Frederick. Business Netiquette International. 20 May 1996. Updated Apr. 1999. Pearman Cooperation Alliance. 1 Dec. 1999 <http://www.bspage.com/1netiq/Netiq.html#TOP>.

Post, Emily. <u>Etiquette: in Society, in Business, in Politics and at Home.</u> New York: Funk & Wagnalls, 1922. Nov. 1999. <u>Bartleby Project.</u> 6 Dec. 1999 <http://www.bartleby.com/95>.

MLA

Using the APA (American Psychological Association) Style

The APA style is used for courses in the social sciences—such as anthropology, economics, psychology, and sociology. The life sciences—such as biology, environmental science, medicine—use a similar style or the numbered system that is described beginning on page 121. Check the requirements for your report.

■ Format for Citations in the Body of Your Paper

The APA style requires that the author's name and the date of original publication be given as information is presented in the body of the paper. If the author's name is given in your sentence, the date appears immediately afterwards, in parentheses. If you have not used the author's name, both last name and date appear in parentheses after the information—usually at the end of the sentence. The respective sources are then presented alphabetically in the list of references at the end of the paper.

Only direct quotations require page numbers. If the article appeared in print first, list those page numbers if possible, even if you read the material online.

In the body of your paper it would look like this:

> Kimberly Jaynes (1998, March–April) reported that only one agency is evaluating distance learning for accreditation.

Your References page will give this listing:

> Jaynes, Kimberly. (1998, March–April). "Dispatch: The Dark Side of Distance Learning." Networker, 8 (4). Retrieved June 6, 1999 from the World Wide Web: http://www.usc.edu/go/ networker/97-98/Mar_Apr_98/ dispatch-distance_learning.html

The "retrieved" date is the date you viewed it. Notice that you do not place a period after the Internet address.

The rationale for the reference list is to provide the details so that the reader can read your source if desired. However, there are times when you will give the complete information for your source in your paper and no additional citation will be required in the reference list.

Personal Communications

Private exchanges cannot be reviewed by your reader. In the body of your paper refer to information from an e-mail, letter, conversation, or interview as a personal communication. Use the

APA

phrase "personal communication" with the date in parentheses after the name.

> Learning disabled students can use the outline view in their word processors to organize even very scattered compositions, according to M. McAllister (personal communication, May 6, 1998).

An Entire Website

When the address is given for a website used as a general reference, no other information is necessary. In the body of your paper, refer to the title of the website and give its address in parentheses.

> Psychcrawler is a search engine devoted to psychological topics (http://www. psychcrawler.com).

■ Format for Listing Sources at the End of Your Paper

Heading: Center the heading, References. Use caps and lowercase, no underline, boldface, italics, or quotation marks.

Sequence: Alphabetize by the last names of the authors. When no author is listed, alphabetize by the first main word of the title. **Do not number the list.**

Spacing: Double-space the entire list with no extra space between entries.

APA

Indentation: Start at the margin for the first line of each entry. Indent the subsequent lines five spaces or half an inch from the left margin.

Authors' Names: Last name, initial(s). Give Jr. if listed, but not M.D. or Ph.D. Reverse all the authors' names if there are several—up to six. With six or more authors, list the first and then write et al., meaning "and others."

When the same author has written more than one work, give the full name of the author each time, and list the works in reverse chronological order—most recent date first. To distinguish two or more works by the author(s) for the same date, list them alphabetically by title, placing *a* after the alphabetically first work's copyright date (e.g., 1997a), *b* after the second (1997b), and so on. Then in your parenthetical citations, the date plus letter will clearly identify the work.

Dates

For date of publication, list year, month day—with a comma after the year. Spell out all months in full. For date of retrieval, list month day, year—with no extra comma after the year.

Titles

Capitalize only the first word of titles and subtitles plus any proper names. Underline titles of main works—books, newspapers, websites, and CD-ROMs. List first the titles of shorter works that appear inside the larger ones—such as file names, articles, stories, chapters, and sections.

APA

■ Guidelines for Specific Sources

Standalone Database or CD-ROM

Author or organization. (original publication date). "Title." (or the heading of the material you read) <u>Title</u> and publishing information of original in print, if known. Retrieved from <u>Title of the database</u> (publication medium, vendor [if relevant], date).

> Anderson, B. R. (1993, September–October). "Safety Assured." <u>Work Study.</u> 42, 29–30. Retrieved from <u>ABI/Inform</u> database (CD-ROM, 1999).

Print Source Retrieved Online

Author or organization. (Date of publication or last revision). "Title of the article." (if appropriate) <u>Title of the Complete Publication.</u> Pages or publishing information. Retrieved date from the World Wide Web at address of the website

> Kiernan, Vincent. (1999, December 17). "How Egalitarian Societies Rein in Potential Despots." <u>Chronicle of Higher Education.</u> A22. Retrieved December 14, 1999 from the World Wide Web: http://www.chronicle. com?weekly/v46/i17/17a02201.htm

APA

A Specific Document on a Website

Author or organization (if known). (Date of publication or last revision). "Title of the article." <u>Title of the Complete Work</u>. Retrieved date from the World Wide Web: address of the website

> Cooperative Extension Service, Mississippi State University. (1997, June 24). "Fowl Cholera." <u>Bacterial Diseases.</u> Retrieved June 5, 1999 from the World Wide Web: http://www. msstate.edu/dept/poultry/disbact.htm

An Entire Website

In the APA style, give the address of the website in parentheses at the end of your sentence. Do not give the web address in your reference list.

Direct E-Mail to You (Not a Discussion Group)

In the APA style, you do not list any personal communications (e-mails, letters, conversations) in your references because no one else can review the source.

APA

◼ Sample Reference Page, APA Style*

REFERENCES

American Chemical Society. (2000). <u>ACS</u>

<u>publications</u>. Retrieved March 31, 2000 from

the World Wide Web: http://pubs.acs.org

American Psychological Association. (1999,

November 11). <u>Electronic Reference</u>

<u>Formats Recommended by the American</u>

<u>Psychological Association</u>. Retrieved

December 11, 1999 from the World Wide

Web: http://www.apa.org/journals/

webref.html

American Psychological Association. (1994).

<u>1994 Publication Manual of the American</u>

<u>Psychological Association</u>. Washington, DC.

Council of Biology Editors. (1994). <u>Scientific</u>

<u>Style and Format: The CBE Manual for</u>

<u>Authors, Editors, and Publishers</u>. 6th ed.

Washington, DC: American Institute of

Biological Sciences.

APA

Also the reference page for Part 4.

Gibaldi, Joseph. (1999). <u>MLA Handbook for
Writers of Research Papers</u>. 5th ed. New
York: Modern Language Association.

Harnack, A., and G. Kleppinger.
(1996, June 10). <u>Beyond the MLA Handbook:
Documenting Electronic Sources on the
Internet</u>. Retrieved April 1, 2000 from
the World Wide Web: http://english.
ttu.edu/Kairos/1.2/inbox/mla_archive.html

Modern Language Association.
(1998, July 9). <u>How to Cite Electronic
Information</u>. Retrieved December 12, 1999
from the World Wide Web: http://www.mla.
org/set_stl.htm

University of Chicago Press.
(1993). <u>Chicago Manual of Style</u>. 14th ed.
Chicago: University of Chicago Press.

Walker, J., and T. Taylor. (1998). <u>The Columbia
Guide to Online Style</u>. New York: Columbia
University Press.

APA

Using the Chicago Manual Style (Footnotes or Endnotes)

Use footnotes or endnotes for professional writing, for cross-disciplinary courses, and for courses in business and law.

The footnote or endnote system is the least intrusive of all types of citations, but it is not as popular among college instructors nowadays. Nevertheless, this classic system is still preferred by some teachers and many publications, and it is ideal for a general audience. Consider using footnotes or endnotes when you don't want to sound stuffy but still need to give some references—for example, for an article for a community newsletter or for your own website. However, check with your teacher before using this style for an academic paper.

■ Format for Citations in the Body of Your Paper

When you use footnotes or endnotes, you give a superscript (raised) numeral each time you present information in the body of the paper. After the fact or quotation, the number cues the reader that there

Chic

is a reference—at the bottom of the page (footnote) or at the end of the paper (endnote).

Computers simplify this system of presenting sources. In most word-processing programs, indicate where you want the number to be inserted, specify whether you want a footnote or endnote, and then type the content of each note as you go through the documentation of your paper. The computer will automatically format the notes and keep track of your sequence of numbers during both composition and revision.

Start numbering consecutively, beginning with the number *one* after the first presentation of research information. Use a different number for each presentation of information (regardless of whether the source is the same or different). In the body of your paper, it would look like this:

> Caroline Link, director of <u>Beyond Silence,</u> does not know sign language; she used an interpreter for communicating with the deaf actors.[2]

The reader of your paper could then look for the corresponding number (2) at the bottom of the page for your footnote or turn to the endnotes at the end of the paper where you have listed the complete reference.

2. Nina Davidson. "Thursday Art Attack: 'Beyond Silence' Director Caroline Link." <u>Hollywood Online.</u> 4 June 1998. [Cited 1 March 2000]. Available from the World Wide Web <http://www.hollywood.com/news/roundtable/Thursday/06-04-98/>.

Chic

The bibliographical reference, alphabetized by authors' last names, gives the same information in a slightly different format. Often you can omit this list.

> Davidson, Nina. "Thursday Art Attack: 'Beyond Silence' Director Caroline Link." <u>Hollywood Online.</u> 4 June 1998. [Cited 1 March 2000]. Available from the World Wide Web <http://www.hollywood.com/news/roundtable/Thursday/06-04-98/>.

■ FORMAT FOR LISTING SOURCES AT THE END OF YOUR PAPER

Check with your teacher. Since all of the information is in the footnotes or endnotes, a separate list is often superfluous. However, lengthy papers and those published on the Web should have a source list at the end.

Call your list of sources *Bibliography*. Follow the format on page 88 for MLA, with these modifications:

- Surround the date you viewed the document with square brackets [ ] and add the word "Cited".

- Precede the Web address with the phrase "Available from the World Wide Web".

USING THE COLUMBIA ONLINE STYLE

This style is the most comprehensive and logical for reporting electronic sources.

The Columbia documentation style provides a system for presenting electronic sources that the other documentation styles do not address. For consistency, some instructors prefer the Columbia style for listing all sources. Other instructors may prefer that you adapt the directions for the Columbia style for a source that is not covered by your assigned style.

For example, if you are following the guidelines for the MLA or *Chicago Manual* style, check the listings under "humanities" in this chapter. If you are following the guidelines for the APA or CBE style, check the listings under "sciences" in this chapter. Note that, to be consistent with your assigned style, you will need to modify the directions here—for example, by rearranging the order within each entry, by underlining rather than italicizing, or by adding angle brackets.

COS

◼ FORMAT FOR CITATIONS IN THE BODY OF A PAPER IN THE HUMANITIES

After the fact or quotation, give, in parentheses, the last name of the author of the source plus the number(s) of the paragraph(s) or screen(s) if designated. Afterward, within the same paragraph, the appropriate paragraph or screen number in parentheses is sufficient.

If no author or organization is listed, give the filename or a brief form of the title in parentheses.

If no paragraph or screen number is given, you will need to repeat the name or title—either in your sentence or in parentheses whenever you present further information from that source.

> Crista Earl and Jay Leventhal praise Qualcomm's Eudora e-mail program as "speech-friendly" because the visually impaired can use the keyboard alone for working within the program.

The reader of your paper could then turn to the *Works Cited* or *Bibliography* where you have listed the complete reference. (The first date is the date of copyright or latest revision. The date in parentheses is the date you viewed it.)

> Earl, Crista, and Jay D. Leventhal. "How Speech Programs Work." *Nature*. 18 Feb. 1999. http://www.nature.com/nature/software (21 Oct. 1999).

COS

■ Format for Listing Sources at the End of a Humanities Paper

Heading: Center the heading, Works Cited (MLA) or Bibliography (Chicago and Columbia). Use caps and lowercase, without underline, boldface, italics, or quotation marks.

Sequence: Make one list, not separated by type of source. Alphabetize by the last names of the authors. When no author is listed, alphabetize by the first main word of the title. Include *a, an* or *the,* but ignore these words when alphabetizing. **Do not number the list.**

Spacing: Double-space the entire list with an extra line space between entries.

Indentation: Start the first line of each entry at the left margin. Indent subsequent lines for that entry five spaces or half an inch (hanging indent). End each entry with a period. *Note:* for electronic publication, block format is acceptable if your browser does not allow for the hanging indent; do not use the tab or return key.

Authors' Names: Reverse authors' names: last name, first name. Give initials or Jr. if listed, but not M.D. or Ph.D. If the author is an organization, give its title without "the."

> Jamiesen, Brendan, Jr.

> National Coalition for the Homeless.

COS

Reverse only the first author's name if there are several. With four or more authors, list the first and then write et al., meaning "and others."

> Brooks, Veronica, and David Ennis.
>
> Pond, Sarah, et al.

When the same author has written more than one work, give the author's full name only for the work that is first in alphabetical order. Then use three hyphens and a period in place of the author's name as you list each of the other works.

> National Council for the Homeless. "Statement on Census 2000 Service Based Enumeration." http://nch.ari.net/census2000.html (28 Mar. 2000).
>
> ---. "Why Are People Homeless?" June 1999. http://nch.ari.net/causes.html (19 Oct. 1999).

Titles: Italicize titles of main works—books, newspapers, multifile websites, and CD-ROMs. List first and use quotation marks around the titles of shorter works that appear inside the larger ones—such as filenames, articles, stories, chapters, and sections. Note that sometimes the entire website may not have a title.

> Shira. "Middle Eastern Music: An Introduction." *The Art of Middle Eastern Dance.* 1 Feb. 2000. http://www.shira.net/musicintro.htm (30 Mar. 2000).

Dates: List day month year with no commas. Abbreviate all months but May, June, and July. List both the date of the original copyright or posting as well as the date you viewed the source, unless you are certain that it is an unchanging source, such as a CD-ROM or video.

Internet Addresses: The item prior to the Internet address should be followed by a period. Give the complete Internet address, including any paths or directory for that specific file.

■ GUIDELINES FOR SPECIFIC SOURCES IN THE HUMANITIES

Standalone Database (CD–ROM) or Other Software

Author (if given). "Title." (or the heading of the material you read) *Title* and publishing information of original in print, if known. *Title of the database.* Publication medium. City of publication and vendor (if relevant), electronic publication date.

> "East Asian Arts: Music Before and Through the Nara Period." *Encyclopedia Britannica CD.* CD-ROM. Chicago: Britannica, 1999.

Online Source (Website, Gopher, Telnet, or FTP)

Nowadays, almost all Internet sources are web-based. In the unlikely event that the information is at a telnet, gopher, or ftp site, the address would begin with the appropriate protocol name rather than http.

COS

Author or organization (if known). "Title of the Document." *Title of the Site* (if different). Date of publication or last revision (if given). Complete address, including any paths or directories (date you viewed it).

> U.S. Dept. of Transportation. "Journey-to-Work Trends in the United States and Its Major Metropolitan Areas 1960–1990." 1996. http://www.bts.gov/NTL/DOCS/473.html (14 July 1999).

Article from an Online Database or Electronic Publication

Author. "Title of the Article." *Title of Publication* (if given). Any identifying information, such as volume number, date, and pages of print version. File number. *Name of database* (if different from the publication). *Name of the online service or Internet address* (date of access).

> Lithwick, Dahlia. "Supreme Court Dispatches: Search and Squeeze." *Slate* 29 Feb. 2000. http://www.slate.com (1 Mar. 2000).

E–Mail, Message Boards, and Discussion Groups

Author (full name if known, otherwise, screen name). "Subject Reference Line." Date of the message if different from date read. *Name and address of group* [if applicable; do not give personal e-mail addresses] (date of access).

Hoffman, Andy. "Cronenberg Leading a Digital eXistenZ." *Brunico Communications Playback.* Toronto International Film Festival page 9, 11 Sept. 1998. *Presswire. Nexis Lexis* (30 Mar. 2000).

J. J. "Re: Freedom of Expression." 10 Feb. 2000. *Alt.Freedom.* (3 Mar. 2000).

Moore, Lisa. "Re: Screen Shots." 10 Feb. 2000.

A sample Works Cited page follows.

COS

■ SAMPLE WORKS CITED, COLUMBIA HUMANITIES STYLE

WORKS CITED

Good, C. Edward. "An E-Mail Education."
Trial, 35 (Feb. 1999): 28 Infotrac.
File # A53913326 (26 Mar. 2000).

"Online Buffs Hit and Miss on Manners."
U.S. News Online. 22 Mar. 1999.
http://www.usnews.com/usnews/issue/
990322/22beha.htm (3 Dec. 1999).

Pearce, Frederick. Business Netiquette
International. 20 May 1996. Updated
Apr. 1999. http://www.bspage.com/
1netiq/Netiq.html#TOP (1 Dec. 1999).

Post, Emily. Etiquette: in Society, in
Business, in Politics and at Home.
New York: Funk & Wagnalls, 1922.
Nov. 1999. Bartleby Project. http://
www.bartleby.com/95 (6 Dec. 1999).

■ FORMAT FOR CITATIONS IN THE BODY OF A PAPER IN THE SCIENCES

After the fact or quotation, give, in parentheses, the last name of the author of the source, the date, and the number(s) of the paragraph(s) or screen(s) if designated. Afterward, within the same paragraph, the appropriate paragraph or screen number in parentheses is sufficient.

If no author or organization is listed, give the title or filename in parentheses.

If no paragraph or screen number is given, you will need to repeat the name or title—either in your sentence or in parentheses whenever you present further information from that source.

> The fire ant pathogen, *Thelohania solenopsae*, was introduced in an attempt to control the red and black fire ant populations (Vail and Pereira, 1999).

The reader of your paper could then turn to *References* at the end of your paper where you have listed the complete information. (The first date is the date of publication; the second date is the date you viewed it.)

> Vail, K., Pereira, R. (1999–2000). Fire ant research. http://www.amesplantation.org/fireantres.htm (18 Feb. 1999).

COS

■ Format for Listing Sources at the End of a Paper in the Sciences

Heading: Center the heading, References. Use caps and lowercase, without underline, boldface, italics, or quotation marks.

Sequence: Make one list, not separated by type of source. Alphabetize by the last names of the authors. When no author is listed, alphabetize by the first main word of the title. Include *a, an* or *the,* but ignore these words when alphabetizing. **Do not number the list.**

Spacing: Double-space the entire list with an extra line space between entries.

Indentation: Start the first line of each entry at the left margin. Indent subsequent lines for that entry five spaces or half an inch (hanging indent). End each entry with a period. *Note:* for electronic publication, block format is acceptable if your browser does not allow the hanging indent; do not use the tab or return key.

Authors' Names: Reverse authors' names: last name, first initial. Separate multiple authors' names with commas. List the first six authors and write et al. ("and others") if there are more. If the author is an organization, give its title without "the."

Advanced Research Projects Agency.

Almquist, E., & Choi, J.

> Flowers, L., Mullins, C., Gilmartin, A.,
>   Redmond, N., Shears, B., Kintigh, T.,
>   et al.

> Silverman, J.

When an author has written more than one work, list the works in reverse chronological order with the latest first. With multiple authors, list entries in alphabetical order by the authors' last names in sequence, but also in reverse chronological order.

> Hegarty, E., Yood, J. (2000).

> Hegarty, E., Sanchez, G., Yood, J. (1999).

> Hegarty, E. (1998).

Titles: Capitalize only the first word and any proper names in titles and subtitles. Italicize titles of main works—books, newspapers, journals, multifile websites, and CD-ROMs. List first the titles of shorter works that appear inside the larger ones—such as filenames, articles, stories, chapters, and sections. Note that sometimes the entire website may not have a title.

Dates: After the author (or title if no author is listed), give, in parentheses, the date of latest copyright or posting—year, month day. Do not abbreviate the month. At the end of the citation, give the date you viewed the source, also in parentheses. List day month year with no commas. Abbreviate all months but May, June, and July. Do not give the date of viewing if you are certain that it is an unchanging source, such as a CD-ROM or video.

COS

Internet Addresses: The item prior to the Internet address should be followed by a period. Give the complete Internet address, including any paths or directory for that specific file.

■ Guidelines for Specific Sources in the Sciences

Standalone Database (CD-ROM) or Other Software

Author (if given). (electronic publication date). Title. (or the heading of the material you read) *Title* and publishing information of original in print, if appropriate. *Title of the database.* Publication medium. City of publication and vendor (if relevant).

> Fire ant. (1999). *Encyclopaedia Britannica CD.* CD-ROM. Chicago: Britannica.

Website or Other Online Source (Gopher, Telnet, or FTP)

Nowadays, almost all Internet sources are web-based. In the unlikely event that the information is at a telnet, gopher, or ftp site, the address would begin with the appropriate protocol name rather than http.

Author or organization (if known). (date of publication or last revision). Title of the document. *Title of the site* (if different).

COS

Complete address, including any paths or directories (date you viewed it).

Office of Highway Information Management. (1999, August 9). Highway statistics 1997. http://www.fhwa.dot.gov/ohim/hs97/hs97page.htm (13 July 1999).

Article from an Online Database or Electronic Publication

Author. (date of publication). "Title of Article." *Title of publication* (if given). Any identifying information, such as series number, date of report. *Name of database* (if different from the publication). *Name of the online service or Internet address* (date you viewed it).

Brown, Jovana. (1999). Salmon Tribes and hydropower dams in Puget Sound. *Fourth world journal.* http://www.cwis.org/fwj/41/jbsalmo.html (26 Mar. 2000).

Center on Budget and Policy Priorities. (2000, January 11). Center on budget and policy priorities to hold briefing to discuss income trend report. *US Newswire.* *Nexis-Lexis* (31 Mar. 2000).

Neuman, P., Rowland, D., Puleo, E. (1999). Understanding the diverse needs of the Medicare population: Implications for Medicare reform. *Journal of aging & social policy,* 10, 25pp. *ArticleFirst. OCLC.* (22 Feb. 2000).

COS

E–Mail, Message Boards, and Discussion Groups

Give e-mail as a reference only if you have quoted it in your paper, since the source cannot be verified by others. Do not give personal e-mail addresses; if possible, give the archive address for mailing lists and discussion groups.

Author (full name if known, otherwise, screen name). "Subject reference line." Date of the message only if different from date read. *Name of group.* address [if applicable] (date of access).

Ashwell, M. "Healthcare forum." (10 Feb. 2000).

Kyburz, B. "Drugs and academic writing" (2000, March 31) *Writing Program Administration* WPA-L@asu.edu (1 Apr. 2000).

COS

■ SAMPLE REFERENCES, COLUMBIA SCIENCES STYLE

REFERENCES

Federal Trade Commission. (July 1999). Self-regulation and privacy online: A report to Congress. <u>Intellectual Property Today</u>. http://www.eff.org/pub/Privacy/199907_ftc_online_privacy_report.html (12 Feb. 2000).

Gladwell, M. (4 November 1996). The science of shopping. <u>New Yorker</u>. http://www.gladwell.com/1996_11_04_a_shopping.htm (10 Mar. 2000).

Kruger, J., and Dunning, D. (1999, December). Unskilled and unaware of it: How difficulties in recognizing one's own incompetence lead to inflated self-assessments. <u>Journal of personality and social psychology</u>. 77. 1121–1134. http://www.apa.org/journals/psp/psp7761121.html (13 Mar. 2000).

CBE

Using the CBE or ACS Number System

Both the Council of Biology Editors (CBE) and the American Chemical Society (ACS) endorse the numbered reference system, although the CBE also endorses the author-date system described on pages 96–103. Check with your teacher. This system is used for courses in mathematics, statistics, physics, and chemistry. It may also be specified for other courses in the sciences.

This system assigns a number to each source:

- Sources are numbered according to their order of citation in the paper.

- The same number is then repeated whenever that source is credited for information within the paper.

- In the body of the paper, the numbers are raised (superscript) and placed right after the information.

- In the reference list at the end, the sources are listed in their numerical order.

When two sources are referred to in the paper simultaneously, both numbers are separated by a comma. In your paper, it would look like this:

CBE

A number of "algo-rithmic stand-alone music and picture applications" are available for free download for personal use.[1,2]

Then at the end of the paper, your reader could find the sources for your information.

(1) <u>Abstracts from Files in info-mac/art as of 7/25/99.</u> <http://hyperarchive.lcs.mit.edu/ HyperArchive/Archive_Art_&_Info/00art_abs>.

(2) <Muhenry@eastnet.educ.ecu.edu>.

As of this writing, neither ACS nor CBE has issued format requirements for documenting material from electronic sources. Suggestions are given here, based on their requirements for journal articles.

Most of the time in the sciences, you will cite the print version of the source. These illustrations show material that is only available electronically.

■ Format for Listing Sources at the End of Your Paper

Heading: Center the heading, References. Use caps and lowercase, in boldface.

Sequence: Make one numbered list, giving the sources in the order in which they were cited in your paper.

Spacing: Single-space each entry. Skip a line between entries.

CBE

Indentation: Place the number in boldface at the left margin followed by a period. Tab five spaces or half an inch to begin the entry. Align subsequent lines under the first letter of the author's last name—to make a block format. End each entry with a period.

Authors' Names: Last name, first initial. List all multiple authors, all in reverse order with a semicolon between each. Do not give people's titles, such as Dr.

Titles:

Books. Italicize the titles of books, followed by a semicolon. Give the name of the publisher, followed by a colon and two spaces, then the city of publication followed by a comma and one space and the date.

Articles. Do not give the title for articles in journals. Abbreviate and italicize the titles of journals. Give the year, boldfaced or underlined with a wavy line, followed by a space, and then the volume number, no space, the issue number within parentheses, a comma, one space and then the complete page numbers.

Dates: Give the year only. Boldface the year for journals but do not do so for books.

CBE

PART 5

A GUIDE FOR BEGINNERS

CONNECTING TO THE INTERNET

You can connect to the Internet, sometimes for free.

The Internet is the name given to the network of all the computers in the world that can communicate with each other. The most common means of connection is a modem (an electronic device that uses the telephone lines to transmit the data between computers), but some systems use cable or satellites. There are a number of ways that you can get access to the Internet, many of them low-cost or even free:

- From home if you have an account and the necessary software from your college, library, office, or online service.

- At a library where Internet access is available at designated computers.

- At a college computer lab with Internet access.

- At a workplace where Internet access is available at designated computers. Note that workplace connections are not private; e-mail and search histories may be reviewed by the employer.

- At a commercial outlet (perhaps called "Internet Cafe" or "Cyberhouse") where you can use computers for an hourly fee—check the yellow pages of your local directory under "Computer Rental" or "Computer Training." These places ordinarily have technical advisers, and many offer classes in using the Internet. Be aware that even though the outlet may offer access to online commercial services, you can't use one without your own established personal account.

Note: Information is also available on computers if you have an encyclopedia or other resource on CD-ROM. A CD-ROM is a disk that looks just like an audio CD, but it contains computer programs or data—often the equivalent of whole shelves of books or periodicals. CD-ROM versions of encyclopedias, dictionaries, atlases, and other reference works are available in libraries and also for consumer purchase. Sometimes you are connecting to a CD-ROM on the Internet. *ROM* means "Read Only Memory" since the data on a CD-ROM is fixed (can't be changed), unlike the fluidity of most information you encounter online.

You are not online when you are using a non-networked computer for word processing or for reading a CD-ROM. The term *online* means that the computer you are using is communicating with another computer, for example, to connect to the Internet or to access a library's regularly updated catalog and other resources.

■ Equipment Needed to Connect to the Internet

If you want to use the Internet from home, you will need:

- A computer with at least 32 megabytes of memory and a Pentium processor, a monitor, a keyboard, and a mouse.

- A modem (at least 28,800 speed; 56K is preferred), plus communications software to use it.

- A phone line or a cable connection if your college or building provides it.

- Additional software depending on what your Internet server requires.

Optional Equipment (Recommended for the World Wide Web)

- A color monitor.

- A sound card and speakers.

- Multimedia software if you want to use multimedia sources.

Regardless of the method of connecting to the Internet, the computer you use is communicating (via modem, cable, or satellite) with a powerful computer (the *server*) that is in turn connected to the Internet. From your personal computer or workstation, you use computer software that communicates with the server computer. (Ordinarily, that software is provided when you get an Internet account to use at home—either with your college, library, or workplace, or with a commercial service). Other software programs in the server allow you to use e-mail (electronic mail), browse the Web, or download files from the Internet to your disk. Because you are dealing with a computer between you and the Internet, high usage may tax the system you are using, causing slowdowns or even crashes.

Internet Accounts: Username and Password

In order to receive e-mail, you will need an Internet account. Your college or public library may offer free accounts, or you can sign up for free e-mail offered by a number of sites (see page 191). For a monthly fee, you can get an account with a commercial service, such as America Online, Microsoft Network, or AT&T.

When you open an Internet account, you will be asked to submit a *username* and *password* so you can *logon* and receive *e-mail.* The username (*ID* or *userid*) plus your server's address will be your *e-mail address* on the Internet (usually username@server address, such as wienbrd@sunynassau.edu). Sometimes you won't get your first choice of username—because someone else is already using it, or because your server assigns usernames by an established system.

Your password is the sequence of letters or numbers (or better, a combination of letters and numbers) that you type in to gain access to your account. Since you'll be using it often, select one that is easy to remember and quick to type—and one that others won't be likely to guess. Be sure to type both your username and password carefully during the initial setup, because what you type is the only sequence the computer will recognize ever after; and write both down in a safe location, not in your computer files.

UNDERSTANDING INTERNET ADDRESSES

The Internet address tells you what kind of institution is there.

The Internet address (sequence of letters and numbers you type to send e-mail or to reach another computer on the Internet) is based on an established system, DNS (Domain Name System). The last three digits designate the type of institution at the Internet address:

.edu is used by educational institutions.

.org is used by non-profit organizations.

.gov is used by governmental agencies.

.mil is used by the military.

.com is used by commercial organizations.

.net is used by large computer networks.

These addresses assume that the site is in the United States. In addition, you may encounter addresses that end in a two-letter country code. Here are a few:

AT—Austria	GR—Greece
AU—Australia	IL—Israel
BR—Brazil	IT—Italy
CA—Canada	JP—Japan
CH—Switzerland	KR—Korea
DE—Germany	MX—Mexico
ES—Spain	UK—United Kingdom
FR—France	US—United States

You can also figure out some addresses for websites; try a simple name with the appropriate prefix and suffix.

For example, you can reach these websites by typing their fairly obvious addresses:

Earthwatch	http://www.earthwatch.org
FAA	http://www.faa.gov
New York Times	http://www.nytimes.com

When visiting a site via a link, you can erase the later file connections in the address to get to the main page. For example, suppose you came across an article on "liver function" with this address:

http://sadieo.ucsf.edu/alf/alffinal/progregen.html

You could delete everything after .edu and send your browser to this address:

http://sadieo.ucsf.edu

There you would find links to the staff and Liver Center at the University of California at San Francisco, with additional links to "other sites of interest"—great sources for topics related to the human liver.

Typing Online

Type carefully when you are online because a mistake can take you to the wrong location or to nowhere at all.

If you know you typed correctly, be aware that the Internet changes rapidly. Use the directories and search engines on pages 169+ and 182+ to check addresses.

In general,

- Check each character before pressing Enter/Return.

- Use no spaces with Internet addresses.

- Use no period at the end (there may be a slash /).

- Use lowercase unless told that the program is "case sensitive" or if you are copying an obvious capital in an Internet address.

- Use the shift key (not the CapsLock key) for the upper symbol on the number or punctuation keys.

- Be careful to distinguish between the letter L and the number 1, and between the hyphen - and the underline _ (which is above the hyphen).

- The ~ symbol is the Spanish tilde, above the grave accent(`), at the top left of the keyboard.

- Slashes (diacritical marks //) are forward slashes, at the bottom right of the keyboard.

- The Break key is also called Pause; it's on the top right of the keyboard, above Page Up.

- On the Macintosh, Ctrl is open ⌘ apple and Alt is closed apple.

GETTING AROUND WITHIN DIFFERENT COMPUTER PROGRAMS

Regardless of the program you're using on your own computer, you will be restricted to the format of the program you're communicating to on the Internet.

Even if you've used a computer for word processing, you may encounter computer systems in the library or on the Internet where your actions will not bring about the expected results.

Using the Keyboard Only

DOS and UNIX systems are character- or text-based, responding only to commands that are typed in. You will need to pay attention to the directions on each screen, because programs ask you to use different keys at different times. Sometimes you will

- Type the number of the item you want.

- Type the highlighted letter of the item.

- Type the word or phrase; press Enter/Return.

- Using an arrow or tab key, highlight the item; press Enter/Return.

Usually, the directions will appear at the bottom of the screen, but sometimes, you'll be "prompted" by a blinking cursor right on the line where you should type. If nothing happens after you have typed something, press Enter/Return.

You can also use your keyboard instead of the mouse for navigating around mouse-based websites. Just use the arrow keys to reach the phrase you want, and then press the Enter/Return key to select the phrase.

Using the Mouse

Windows and Macintosh systems use design and pictures (graphics) in addition to words to tell the computer what to do. With a mouse-based program, you mouse-click on highlighted phrases in the text or on icons (little symbolic pictures). You will then either press a key, or mouse-click, or type in what you want. As you are working within a program, you will notice various borders that outline "windows" on the screen. You open and close these windows as you move through the program.

If you've never used a mouse before, practice with it before going online. Move the mouse around on the pad until the cursor (arrow or vertical bar) on the screen is positioned on the icon or phrase you want to select; then click once (press the upper portion of the mouse, close to the wire—if there are two "buttons" to press, press the left one). You will see your selection highlighted on the screen. When you have to type in a line, position the cursor on the left margin of the space where the first letter should go, and then click the mouse before you type.

Maneuvers—with Either Keyboard or Mouse

Selecting. Often you will tell the computer what you want by choosing from a *menu* (list) of options or by selecting an underlined phrase presented in a different color from the rest of the text. You communicate your selection by clicking the mouse or by pressing Enter/Return after the choice is highlighted. Note that a phrase can't be selected until the cursor is positioned *exactly* on the phrase; with many programs, the cursor changes from an arrow to a hand pointing upward to indicate that you can select at that point.

Scrolling. To scroll (move vertically through the text) you can use the arrow keys, the Page Up or Page Down keys, or the mouse. To use the mouse, look at the right margin of the innermost window frame. Either position the cursor and click continuously on the arrow pointing in the direction you want to move the text (up or down), or click on the "button" to slide it down the margin as you read. Just click and hold the mouse as you guide it smoothly and in a straight line (toward you to go down; away from you to go up). This method is particularly useful if you want to skim a document quickly. That "button" in the right margin is also a clue to the length of the material you are reading; it will slide down to the bottom margin as you approach the end of the document.

You won't be able to scroll through or save a document while it is loading. Programs usually provide a visual clue to the status of downloading—for example, with a horizontal bar graph, a thermometer, shooting stars (Netscape), or a pulsating pyramid (America Online).

Other Options. The headings in each program vary, but there are usually a number of other useful options listed on the top of the screen. If you highlight them there will either be an explanation or a drop-down menu (mouse-click on the heading; then, while holding the mouse "button" down, drag down to highlight your choice; release the mouse). In some programs, you move through the menu with arrows and then press Enter/Return when you reach the one you want. See the next page for definitions of the Bookmark, Reload, Forward, Back, Stop, and History "buttons."

Error Messages. Many programs will alert you with a sound effect if you're trying to perform something that won't work. Others will give an error message. You can usually click on *Help* (or type h or ?) to learn what to do.

Exit. As you enter a program, often there will be a line at the beginning telling you how to exit or quit. Note that command (frequently Alt + F4). If you forget, you can usually type Q or mouse-click in the top-right or top-left corner where you'll see an X or square. **Don't just turn off your computer—** particularly if you're connected to a text-based host computer program. It can leave that computer line busy for others.

Traveling Around Websites

Just click with your mouse to tell your browser where to go on the Web.

After you have visited a number of different websites, you may want to retrace your path. When you are at any site, you can click on "buttons" on the margins of the page you're looking at. To get the description of each "button," point your mouse to the name or picture (icon). Mouse-click on the "button" to tell your browser what to do.

- **Back** takes you to the previous webpage.

- **Forward** takes you to the next page that you visited after the present one, but only after you've first moved backward.

- **Reload** or **Refresh** gets a better image of the website back on your screen.

- **Bookmark** saves the address of the website to your list (also called "go" or "favorites").

- **Home** takes you to the homepage of your server—your college, library, or online service.

- **History** lists the sites already visited.

- **Stop** interrupts downloading or the attempt to reach a site, necessary during a slowdown.

- The **X** or **square** in the top right-hand corner of the screen (or top-left for Mac) allows you to exit quickly—usually returning to your homepage, but sometimes signing you off.

UNDERSTANDING HOW INFORMATION IS STORED

More and more information that is suitable for academic papers is available through the Internet.

If you have Internet service on your home computer, you can do much of your research for a report right there. This is particularly true if you have the software for using an account with your college or public library and thus have access to library subscriptions to specialized databases. Find out if any passwords are necessary for accessing these specialized sources from home. A list of suggested databases appears in the appendix of this book.

■ FIND THE INFORMATION YOU WANT

Using computers to find information sounds easy, and often it is. However, you will also have access to much more material than you could ever read, and the information you need may be buried under a lot of stuff you don't care about. Keep in mind the fact that information you're looking for has been put there in two ways:

- By a human being who has a logic that may be very different from yours and who can sometimes make mistakes or omissions.

- By a robot that matches every word regardless of context.

Researching with computers can be successful only when you understand how the information is organized and what computers can and cannot do.

■ Use Search Tools

Whether you are searching on CD-ROM or on the Internet, *search tools* (computer programs that locate sources of information) will ask you to select a subject area or to type in search terms (keywords). Search tools operate in three different ways as they try to match your request:

- They try to find your keywords in their collection of information (database) by checking **each title plus the list of keywords** for the website or article as supplied by the author (or sometimes by a researcher at the search tool company). Note that the keywords the author has supplied may not actually be in the article but are submitted as relevant descriptions.

- They look at **every word in every document** in their database for matches to the words you've supplied.

- They look through an **index that a researcher has compiled** of articles or websites in their database that best match the words you have supplied.

Indexers use standard phrases established by the Library of Congress—subject headings—under which all relevant articles are listed. For example, articles related to cooking are listed under "cookery." Some search tools will correct your request for "cooking" by giving you all the articles and websites under "cookery," but others may not. Similarly, some search tools may automatically add synonyms to requests for certain words to enhance the results you get to your query.

However, some commercially motivated individuals supply multiple copies of their websites so their increased number of keywords will attract more visitors to their site. You may need to anticipate which aspect of your topic has a commercial angle. For example, if you are looking for information on the availability of potable water around the world, a search for "potable water" will first list all the sites that sell bottled water and water purification devices. You will need to add medical terms to your query to get the more scientific websites on water quality worldwide.

Researching programs are constantly being improved to make them better able to interpret what information is being sought, and more websites with information are added each hour, so you'll often get plenty of information quickly. However, you still need to be creative in how you tell the computer what to look for.

Understanding What Computers Can and Cannot Do

Phrasing your question carefully will help you find the right answer.

Computers Can	What You Must Do
Scan a vast number of documents rapidly.	Determine the best words to use for scanning the documents.
Help narrow your search.	Articulate the limits of your search.
Allow you to download files to use in your report.	Save the files on your disk; record bibliographic information.

Computers Cannot	What You Must Do
Violate the rules of their program.	Read helplines to see what the specific rules are.
Find something listed under a different term.	Use synonyms; suggest more general topics; be creative in phrasing your search.
Find something that isn't there.	Recognize that some material isn't available electronically; carefully select the databases you search.

Correct a misspelled word.	Type and proofread carefully; use alternate spelling when appropriate; recognize that typos occur in indexes and catalogs.
Discriminate between different meanings— such as Turkey the country or turkey the bird.	Add words preceded by "not" so you eliminate unwanted usage of your search terms.
Provide context.	Add terms that provide context—such as "turkey wings."

If you feel overwhelmed or frustrated, stop to recall what you asked the computer to do. You may have asked the wrong question, or the answer you expect is not as readily available as you had hoped. You need not be intimidated by the wealth of information on the Internet; you can, with patience, usually find ways to discover what you want to know.

Changing Browsers

You don't have to use the browser your Internet
service provider gives you.

Microsoft's Internet Explorer (MISE) may be the
browser integrated with your Internet provider's
system, as it is with America Online and Microsoft
Systems Network. However, many researchers prefer
Netscape Navigator—Netscape's web browser.

* Netscape Navigator automatically records the
  URL and date of access for any material from
  the Internet that you save or print. You will
  need to write down all information if you use
  Microsoft's Internet Explorer.

* Netscape Navigator allows you to adjust the
  page size of a website before saving or printing.
  With Microsoft's Internet Explorer, try
  changing the printing properties to landscape
  orientation for a page that doesn't fit
  horizontally.

* Netscape Navigator allows you to import your
  bookmark list to any word processing program,
  whereas Microsoft programs will erase any
  addresses they do not recognize.

You can download Netscape Navigator free from
<http://www.netscape.com>. Just connect to the
Internet first; then go to the website and follow the
instructions under "download."

Once Netscape Navigator is installed on your
desktop, you will always need to connect first to
the Internet with your provider, but you can
specify that Netscape be on your homepage. Just
minimize your Internet service provider's screen.
At the end of any session on the Web, close
Netscape first before signing off.

SAVING FILES

Save information from a database or Internet site so you can use it later in your word processing program.

Saving

At the top of the screen, most programs have a section labeled "Options" or "Commands." Mouse-click (or use the arrow and press Enter/Return) to read a menu of choices. *Save* or *Record* will allow you to save the data in the file on your current screen (which you can then read more carefully and extract specific notes) and many programs even give an appropriate footnote.

If you are working in a library or computer lab, be sure to save your notes in text-only format, both to save space and to make sure that your word-processing program can read them. Save an image with a name plus the extension it has, such as *.gif*, *.jpg*, or *.bmp*. Some libraries or computer labs have workstations where you can't save on your own disk; if not, print the files you want, and write down the source information or Internet address on the copy if the program doesn't automatically do so.

- Insert your formatted disk into the appropriate drive.

- Highlight the text or picture you want (if possible, highlight the title and author/creator as well). If the program does not allow you to highlight, then you will be saving the entire file that you can see without clicking on any links.

- Click on "File."

- Drag down to "Save As."

- Name the file. Be sure to name each file with a different name, preferably with the specific subtopic, and write down the full title of the file and its Internet address (because you can't enter any of your own writing directly on this file yet).

- PC users will need to specify which computer drive their disk is in (usually A). If using a Mac, make sure that you are saving to your disk and not to the hard drive.

- If using a PC, give a word file a .rtf (Rich Text Format) or .txt (text) extension; give an image the same extension it already has, such as *.gif*, *.jpg*, or *.bmp*. If using a Mac, save the file as a text-only or image file.

- Click on "Save." **Note that only the file you're actually reading will be saved—not any of the linked files at other web addresses.** If you want them also, you have to get each file on the screen and save each one separately.

Write down or type into your bibliographic file any information—such as title, author, Web address, and the date you viewed it. Most of this information will automatically appear in your file if you are using the Netscape browser. If uncertain, print a copy to see before exiting from the website.

Opening a File in Other Applications

In your word-processing program, you can open a text-only file by asking the program to search "all files." Then you can save it in your favorite format (such as a "Word document") with your default typeface.

To insert an image you have previously saved, first move your cursor to the place you want the image to appear, then:

- With Microsoft Word or PowerPoint, click on "Insert," then "Picture," then the filename, then OK.

- With Word Perfect, select "Open," "filename," "Open."

APPENDICES

GLOSSARY: SOME KEY TERMS

Archives   Historical collection; copies of past issues of magazines and newspapers, often available only for a fee, but also previous messages of a discussion group. Archives are often organized by topic, but sometimes all articles or messages are presented in reverse chronological order. Visiting the archives of a discussion group is essential before joining in any conversation. See also *FAQs*.

Asynchronous   Not at the same time. Mailing lists and most discussion groups have e-mail "conversations" that take place between members of the group who write and read messages according to their own individual schedules. See pages 34+ for further explanation.

Bandwidth   The energy level and percentage of broadcast time used for transmission of data through the airwaves. Telephone, radio, cable, and satellites all use bandwidth. Each has its particular spectrum or transmission area. Any time you are connected to the Internet or talking on your cell phone you are using some bandwidth. Some systems are more efficient than others; for example, cable modems are very fast and allow users to be permanently connected to the Internet. Plain text doesn't require much bandwidth for transmission, but multimedia files do. It's only fair to avoid overburdening the system: Logoff when you have finished surfing. Do your reading and composing of e-mail offline. Send big files only if you're sure the recipient wants them.

Bit   The smallest amount of information understood by a computer. See *byte*.

Blind copy   A copy of a message sent without that addressee's name showing to other recipients. In many programs, just click on "blind copy" in the address book; in other programs, you usually can enclose the blind copy address in parentheses. You will still need to send the message to one visible recipient, but that can be to your own address or to a pseudonym at a free e-mail box. This is a useful way to control spamming since many hackers get addresses from jokes and other messages people keep forwarding without removing the previous list of addressees.

Bookmark   A mechanism that tells your browser to save a particular Internet address for revisiting (called *favorites* in AOL and *history* in Explorer). See page 8 for information on how to bookmark.

Browse   A computer program that views webpages on the Internet.

Byte   A group of eight bits processed as a unit of information, about the size of one character on the typed page. Kilobyte, a thousand bytes; megabyte, a thousand kilobytes; gigabyte, a thousand megabytes.

Cache   The place where your browser stores portions of a website so it reloads images quickly on your next visit. Since the cache is using memory on your hard drive, it's a good idea to empty the cache periodically. However, you should adjust the cache setting to retain information for the duration of your research project.

Case sensitive   Most programs treat capitalized and lowercase letters the same. However, if it makes a difference, you will be advised that the site is "case sensitive," so capitalizing or not will affect the outcome.

CD disk for computers   A disk that looks just like an audio CD, but contains computer programs or data—often the equivalent of shelves full of books or periodicals.

CD-R   Purchased as a blank disk, a CD-R can be recorded on only once. CD-R disks can be played in any CD drives—audio on CD players, audio or data on computer CD drives. Use CD-R or CD-RW drives for recording onto CD-R disks.

CD-ROM   *ROM* means "Read Only Memory" since the data on a CD-ROM is fixed (can't be changed). CD-ROM versions of encyclopedias, dictionaries, atlases, and other reference works are available in libraries and also for consumer purchase. Sometimes you are connecting to a CD-ROM on the Internet.

CD-RW   A CD that can be recorded on and recorded over thousands of times without a compromise in quality. *RW* means "Rewritable"; CD-RW disks can only be played in CD-RW drives, but CD-RW drives can play all kinds of CD disks.

Chat   See *IRC*.

Cookie   A minuscule amount of data left on your hard drive after you visit most websites. The cookie tells the site next time that you are a return visitor, allowing you to bypass introductory pages or registration procedures. Note that some websites read your cookie file to see what other websites you have visited, so some people reject cookies as a matter of privacy.

Cyberspace   The term describing the entire area traversed by electronic communications.

Database   Electronically stored information. Databases can be as small as a simple mailing list or as huge as the collections of libraries or government agencies. Sometimes you can't get the information you want because you're searching the wrong database.

Discussion group, discussion list, newsgroup, or mailing list   A group of people who communicate regularly on a particular topic, via e-mail. See pages 34+ for further explanation.

DNS (Domain Name System)   The address system for reaching sites on the Internet. Both for e-mail and website locations, addresses end with a three-letter designation indicating the type of institution (*edu* for educational institutions; *com* for commercial institutions, and so forth). See page 131 for further explanation.

Download   The method of copying a file from the Internet to your disk or to the hard drive of your computer.

E-mail (electronic mail)   The method of sending messages via computer—either to one person or to a group of people. E-mail makes it possible to send copies simultaneously to a great many people, which is what discussion groups do.

Encryption   The scrambling of data so it cannot be read by outsiders. On the Internet, messages can be intercepted as they travel through cyberspace. Websites where you enter your credit card numbers or other personal data should post a message to assure you that your data will be transmitted safely. Your browser will provide a lock or key icon to indicate that you are at a secure site, and the prefix will often read "https" rather than "http."

Most Internet service providers give a warning that you are about to submit an "insecure" document. If that is the case, others would be able to read your message. By law, a telephone number must be given so that you can phone in your order when you are visiting an insecure site.

Explorer   See *Internet Explorer.*

Export   Copy the current file to another application. When you are working on the Internet, you can save the data to your word-processing program or spreadsheet if all of your programs are the latest by Microsoft or if you are using Netscape. Otherwise, highlight the material and use the "save as" function.

FAQs   Frequently asked questions. A number of informational sites as well as discussion groups list previously answered questions. Always consult the FAQs before submitting your own query. In addition, FAQs are available on specific subjects. Try entering "FAQs" plus your search terms into a search engine to see what comes up.

Favorites   A mechanism in AOL that tells your browser to save a particular Internet address for revisiting (called *bookmark* or *history* in other programs).

Freeware   Software that you can download from the Internet for free.

FTP (File Transfer Protocol)   FTP sites offer files—including programs—that you can download, sometimes for free and often for a fee.

GUI   Pronounced "gooey," it means "graphic user interface," the ability of computer systems to use icons (little pictures) that you click on with your mouse to quickly connect to the innerworkings of the computer. This interface, originated by Xerox, used in all Macintosh computers, and now incorporated into Windows systems, makes it possible to surf the World Wide Web as you click on one link and then another. This method contrasts with the DOS and UNIX systems of typing in words and symbols to tell a computer what to do.

History   A mechanism in Netscape that tells your browser to save a particular Internet address for revisiting (called *favorites* in AOL or *bookmarks* in other programs).

Homepage   A base page on the World Wide Web. Individuals or companies each have their own homepage or main page, which is where most visitors first enter a particular site. Your own homepage can be one you have created for yourself, or it is the opening screen (at either your library, your Internet service provider, or your company website) where you enter the Internet.

HTML (Hypertext Markup Language)   The formatting that programmers use to create documents on the World Wide Web.

http (hypertext transfer protocol)   The method computers use to communicate on the World Wide Web, the opening of every World Wide Web address, followed by a colon (:) and two slashes (//).

Hyperlinks   The images or underlined, differently colored lines of text that you click on to take you to another section of the document you are reading or to another Web address.

Hypertext   Any text connected by hyperlinks, either within documents or online.

Import   Copy a file from another application. When you are working in your word-processing program or spreadsheet, you can import data from the Internet if all of your programs are the latest by Microsoft or if you use the Netscape browser. Otherwise, highlight the material and use the "save as" function.

Internet   The name given to the network of all the computers in the world that can communicate with each other, via modem, cable, or satellite.

Internet Explorer   Microsoft's web browser (MSIE), integrated into many computer systems as well as Internet providers such as America Online and Microsoft Network (MSN).

Internet service provider (ISP)   The means by which you connect to the Internet. See pages 127+ for further explanation.

Intranet   The name given to all the computers that communicate within a closed system—for example, at a business—allowing for sharing of files and other collaborative work. The system users may also have outside access to the Internet, but outsiders do not have access to the shared files of the intranet.

IRC (Internet Relay Chat)   The system that allows for synchronous (same time) "conversations" via typed messages at a particular website. Areas of the conversation are called channels or chat rooms, and participants usually use pseudonyms. Discussions may be moderated or not; any rules for appropriate behavior will be listed at the opening page.

Java   A universal computer programming language—one that can be used by PCs, Macs, DOS, or UNIX systems. Thus it is a key programming language for interactivity on the Web.

Links   See *hyperlinks.*

Listserv   See *discussion groups.*

Loading   The movement of data from one computer to another. Thus a website page is *loading* onto your computer as it gradually comes into view. Note that you can do only a few maneuvers within a file before it is fully loaded, and when you do, you run the risk of crashing your browser.

Logon, logoff   See *online.*

Mailing list   See *discussion groups.*

Message boards   An open system where anyone can post a question or respond to a comment on topics related to the particular named subject. Message boards are often organized by Internet service providers.

Metasearcher   A powerful search engine that searches several search engines at once. See pages 23+ for further explanation.

Modem   An electronic device attached to or inside a computer that uses the telephone lines to transmit the data between computers.

Moderated list   A discussion group where all messages are reviewed before distribution. Messages may be modified, grouped into a "thread" with others, or rejected—depending on the rules of the group.

MOO (MUD object oriented)   An informal, interactive, real-time conversation via typed messages on a website—on a particular topic, where each individual uses a pseudonym and selects a room or channel.

MUD (multiuser dungeon)   An interactive adventure game, that takes place in actual time via typed messages using Telnet or on a website. Each individual uses a pseudonym and plays a role in the game.

Netscape Navigator   Netscape's web browser, which can be used even if you have Internet Explorer integrated with your Internet provider's system. See page 144 for further explanation.

Newsgroups   Officially known as Usenet newsgroups, these are discussion groups you subscribe to, organized around a particular topic, such as rec.food.cooking, which would be devoted to topics related to cooking of food as recreation (leisure). You use a "newsreader" to read articles posted to the group, which will initially be listed by subject line only.

Online   The term for being connected to another computer, where the data you are reading can be modified. The term *online* means that the computer you are using is communicating with another active computer, for example, to connect to the Internet, or to access a library's regularly updated catalog and other resources. To get *online,* you must *logon* (type a password, or go through certain prescribed steps, depending on the system). To go *offline,* you *logoff* (by typing certain words or symbols), or select "sign off" or "quit" from the menu—or close your server to disconnect.

Plug-ins   Small computer programs that enable the browser to use features at given websites, such as sound or video files. Plug-ins, usually available via download and often free for the no-frills versions, reside on your computer and automatically connect when you access a site needing their aid. For example, many sites have sound available, but only if you have installed a version of RealAudio first.

Prompt   Sometimes preceded by a question, the prompt is the spot marked by the blinking cursor or a highlighted space. At the prompt you mouse-click on a button or type in a word or phrase to communicate with the program.

Protocol   A system of electronic rules and format.

Query   The words or phrases that you use to ask a computer program to search its database. Some search tools allow you to ask a question or enter a long string of words. Check the helpline if you are unsure.

Search engine   A program that finds documents or websites for you. A search engine is built into a database on a CD-ROM so that you can call up information stored there, such as an article in an encyclopedia, or a listing in a telephone directory. Search engines on the Web find sites, but even the most powerful can find only a small percentage of what is out there.

Security   On the Internet, messages can be intercepted as they travel through cyberspace. Websites where you enter your credit card numbers or other personal data should post a message to assure you that your data will be transmitted safely. When you are at a secure site, the prefix will read "https" rather than "http." That means that your data will be encrypted (scrambled) so it cannot be read by outsiders.

Most Internet service providers give a warning that you are about to submit an "insecure" document. If that is the case, others would be able to read your message. By law, a telephone number must be given so that you can phone in your order when you are visiting an insecure site.

Server   The high-powered computer where a website or Internet provider is located.

Spamming   The sending of an unsolicited message to a large number of addresses, often for advertising or destructive hacking purposes. You can prevent unsolicited mail by giving your ISP a list of acceptable senders, but this will cut you off from future correspondents you could enjoy hearing from. You can also block specific offenders by asking your ISP to reject any messages from them.

You can help prevent the perpetuation of spamming:

- Avoid sending mass mailings yourself.

- Never open unsolicited mailings, nor reply— even to ask to be removed from the mailing list.

- Don't use your e-mail "forward button."
  Instead, copy and paste any material you want
  to pass on into a new message (without all the
  addresses from the previous sender).

- Send blind copies, rather than listing everyone
  in the "To" box.

- Forward any junk mail to the webmaster of
  your particular service. Most mailing lists and
  Internet service providers have a monitor for
  this purpose; for example, in AOL, it's
  tosspam@aol.com.

Surf   The term for rapid movement from one
website to another. Be sure to bookmark sites while
you are surfing so that you can find your way
back.

Synchronous   At the same time. In chat rooms,
instant messages, MUDs, and MOOs, e-mail
"conversations" take place in current time between
members of the group who write and send
messages rapidly back and forth. See pages 37+ for
further explanation.

Upload   The method of sending a file to the
Internet from a computer.

URL (Uniform Resource Locator)   The unique
address for each Internet site.

> E-mail addresses start with a code for the user's
> name@
>
> FTP sites start with ftp://
>
> Gopher sites start with Gopher://
>
> Websites start with http://

Virus   A malicious program designed to destroy
data or sabotage files. Some viruses will continue
to spread (like an infection), damaging every file or
e-mail message you send thereafter. Viruses arrive

via shared files or downloads, so keep a virus protection program on your computer and update it regularly. Never open files from an unknown source.

Webmaster The manager of a particular website.

Webpage A single item on a larger website. Often a webpage is actually several pages long if printed out. But it is just one segment of a much larger site. (See below.)

Websites Locations on the World Wide Web. The quality and size of websites vary—from simple one-page announcements, to powerful search engines, to multimedia sites, to huge multipage references with links to hundreds of other sites.

World Wide Web (WWW) The interlinked and fastest-growing part of the Internet where you can with one keystroke jump from one topic—and location—to another. As you scroll through the text, you encounter pictures or underlined and differently colored words; when you click your mouse (or press the Enter/Return key) on that phrase, you jump to a different page relevant to that topic. The multimedia sites also include audio (giving, for example, the pronunciation of a word) or video (a film clip).

Worm Like a virus, a worm is a malicious program that destroys data and compromises your computer system. Unlike the virus, which operates like a spreading infection, the worm operates like a tapeworm, expanding and filling all parts of your computer system until the hard drive crashes— often irrevocably. As with viruses, worms arrive through shared files or downloads. Do not open any files you are unsure of.

WWW See *World Wide Web.*

A LIST OF IMPORTANT RESOURCES

Internet addresses listed here are regularly updated on McGraw-Hill's website:

http://www.mhhe.com/writers

Every day, more resources are available online. Your local library may offer software and passwords so you can access major databases free from your home or office; your business organization may provide additional access. But even when a fee is required at a particular site, often it applies only to the ordering of a specific document. You may be able to get what you need by registering and checking the free pages.

The following list does not include printed resources. Although the publication of material is gradually changing from print to digital, there are still important reference materials that are only available in print. Ask a librarian if you don't find what you need here.

There is an advantage to both electronic and print versions; you may prefer to download and print information from a CD-ROM or the Internet, work with it, and then return to the computer. Similarly, you may use both a digital index for rapid selection of material over several years and then consult printed annual indexes for browsing.

■ SUBJECT DIRECTORIES

These websites are organized indexes; you can enter a keyword or you can search by clicking on the topic, then subtopic, then sub-subtopic, and so forth. The advantage is that materials have been organized by human researchers, so most of the results will be relevant. For further explanation, see the chapter beginning on page 10.

About.com   http://www.
                           about.com

(each area is maintained by an expert to whom you can e-mail)

Galaxy   http://galaxy.com

Librarians' Index to the Internet
http://www.lii.org

(an excellent and thorough resource that includes annotations)

Lycos Top 5% of the Web http://point.lycos.com

Magellan   http://magellan.
                           excite.com

(good subject search)

Open Directory Project   http://www.dmoz.org

(a new and very comprehensive directory)

Scout Report Signpost   http://www.
                           signpost.org

(assembled by information specialists)

Subject Area Links   http://webpages.
                           marshall.edu/
                           ~jmullens/subj_areas.
                           html

(links provided by educators)

Yahoo   http://www.yahoo.
                           com

(very fast subject search of a huge database)

■ REFERENCE PAGES

These websites are lists of links to helpful websites, many of which are not found easily via search engines. Also check the websites of textbook publishing houses. For further explanation, see the chapter beginning on page 12.

GENERAL AND LIBRARY REFERENCE PAGES

In addition to the websites listed here, check the homepages of search engines and click on "reference" or on the category for your topic.

The Argus Clearinghouse	http://www.clearinghouse.net
CMC Information Services	http://www/december.com/cmc/info

(formerly December list, it lists search engines and provides links to a variety of helpful resources)

Electric Library	http://www.elibrary.com

(personal edition—free use for 30 days)

Internet Public Library's Ready Reference Collection	http://www.ipl.org/ref/RR
Librarian's Guide to Best Information on the Web	http://www.sau.edu/CWIS/Internet/Wild/index.htm
Library of Congress Research Tools	http://lcweb.loc.gov/rr/tools.html
My Virtual Reference Desk	http://www.refdesk.com

Research-It	http://www.itools.com/research-it/research-it.html
UCB Internet Resources by Subject	http://www.lib.berkeley.edu/Collections/acadtarg.html
The Webmaster's Reference Library	http://www.webreference.com/
WWW Virtual Library	http://conbio.rice.edu/vl/database
World Lecture Hall	http://www.utexas.edu/world/lecture

(faculty websites, organized by discipline)

SUBJECT-ORIENTED REFERENCE PAGES

Art

California Digital Image Finding Aids	http://www.oac.cdlib.org:28008/dynaweb/ead/calher
Digital Images	http://sunsite.berkeley.edu/FindingAids/dynaweb/calher/arbor/figures/I0025 924A.jpg
The World Wide Web Virtual Library Museum	http://palimpsest.stanford.edu/icom/vlmp

Biology/Environment/Health Sciences

Biomedical Meta Websites	http://www.library.ucsf.edu/kr/meta.html

Envirolink   http://envirolink.org

Environmental Organization   http://www.
Web Directory   webdirectory.com

Business and Technology

Business and Technology   http://www.brint.
Knowledgement Showcase   com/brintbook

Guide to Business   http://www.bizweb.
on the Web   com

Education

Edlinks   http://webpages.
                                      marshall.edu/
                                      ~jmullens/edlinks.html

Online Educational   http://quest.arc.nasa.
Resources   gov/OER

Law

FindLaw   http://www.findlaw.
                                      com

Law Facts   http://www.lawguru.
                                      com

Government and History

Federal Information   http://www.
Network   fedworld.gov

Hyper History Timelines   http://www.
                                      hyperhistory.com

Politics1	http://politics1.com
Policy	http://www.policy.com
Public Agenda	http://www./publicagenda.org
Thomas	http://thomas.loc.gov
(U.S. Congress on the Internet)	
Vote Smart	http://www./vote-smart.org

Humanities

Humanities Research	http://humanitas.ucsb.edu

Literature

British and Irish Authors	http://lang.nagoya-u.ac.jp/~matsuoka/UK-authors.html
English Literature	http://lang.nagoya-u.ac.jp/~matsuoka/EngLit.html
The English Server at Carnegie Mellon University	http://english-server.hss.cmu.edu
Literary Locales	http://www.sjsu.edu/depts/english
Literary Resources on the Web	http://andromeda.rutgers.edu/~jlynch/Lit
Pilot Search	http://www.pilot-search.com

(literary search engine)

VOS English Literature
Page
http://humanitas.
ucsb.edu/shuttle/
english.html

Wisdom
http://www.
thinkers.net

(author and literature search)

Psychology

PsychCrawler
http://www.
psychcrawler.com

■ METASEARCHERS, WHICH SIMULTANEOUSLY CHECK FOR YOUR TERMS AMONG SEVERAL SEARCH ENGINES

For an explanation of metasearchers, see the chapter beginning on page 22. For an explanation of search terms, see the chapter beginning on page 14.

If you have developed a good list of search terms, the most effective way to begin is with one of these metasearchers:

Dogpile
http://www.dogpile.
com

(fun to use, it simultaneously searches 25 search engines)

Highway 61
http://www.
highway61.com

(very fast, it searches the six most popular search engines and arranges the results by relevance)

Inference Find   http://www.infind.
                                com

(also very fast and concept oriented, it searches the six top search engines and organizes the results)

SavvySearch   http://savvysearch.
                                com

(fast and thorough)

USE IT!   http://www.he.net/
                                ~kamus/useen.htm

(a unified search engine for InTernet—in Italy, includes international sites)

■ Lists of Search Engines

Includes most of those listed individually on pp. 171+, with links to each. For an explanation of how to use search engines, see pages 22–25.

Internet browsers and library homepages provide lists with links to search engines (so you don't have to type the addresses), but you may want to try the pages in the list here. Alternatively, you can type the URL address given below for individual search engines.

All in One Search Page   http://www.albany.
                                net.allinone

Argus Clearinghouse   http://www.
                                clearinghouse.net

Beaucoup!   http://beaucoup.com

c|net   http://www.search.
                                com

■ POWERFUL SEARCH ENGINES

AltaVista
(one of the most
comprehensive, it also
has a very good subject
directory and accepts
questions; use the
advanced search for
phrases)

http://www.altavista.com

Excite
(large database;
includes summaries,
sorted by relevance
to the topic; offers
"more like this")

http://www.excite.com

FastSearch
(fastest)

http://www.alltheweb.com

Google

http://www.google.com

HotBot
(very large database; fast
and comprehensive;
excellent for multimedia
topics)

http://www.hotbot.com

Iatlas

http://www.iatlas.com

InfoSeek

http://www.infoseek.com

(very fast; best for simple searches; also good for
refining searches)

Lycos

http://www.lycos.com

(oldest and still one of the best; good for searching
for images and sound files)

Search	http://search.cnet.com
Skworm Search (new; has a number of specialized sources in its database—such as *TeenHoopla*)	http://www.skworm.com
NorthernLight (currently the most thorough of the search engines; provides folders for organizing your search; also identifies the date of original posting—often not given on the website—and whether a site is a personal page, commercial, or nonprofit; retrieves some documents for a fee)	http://www.northernlight.com
WebCrawler (one of the fastest)	http://www.webcrawler.com
WorldWideWorm (good for simple searches)	http://www.goto.com

■ INDEXES AND OTHER DATABASES IN LIBRARIES

For an explanation of indexes and databases, see the chapter beginning on page 26. For an explanation of search terms, see the chapter beginning on page 14.

Databases listed here may appear in a menu of choices on your library's homepage, or they may be installed in designated computers in the reference area. If connecting from home, you may need to enter a password to use certain databases, if your library subscribes.

INDEXES

Business Index

ERIC (educational resources)

Humanities Citation Index

Humanities Index

Infoline

InfoTrac

Magazine Index

Medline

Periodicals Index

Science Citation Index

Science Index

Social Science Citation Index

Social Science Index

Westlaw

MULTI-SEARCH DATABASES

ABI-Inform

FirstSearch

Nexis-Lexis

SOME FREE DATABASES ON THE INTERNET

Indexes

The Big Hub	http.//www. the bighub.com
CARL	http://uncweb. carl.org

(Colorado Alliance of Research Libraries; best for academic topics—you don't have to register; the search is free, with copies of articles available for a fee)

ERIC (educational resources)	http://ericir.syr.edu
Internet Oracle	http://www. searchgateway.com
Lycos Searchable Databases	http://dir.lycos.com/ Reference/Searchable_ Databases
Medline	http://www.ncbi.nlm. nih.gov/PubMed http://www. healthgate.com

Statistical Sources

American Statistical Index (also on CD-ROM; a monthly index of all U.S. government statistical publications; see also individual federal agencies' websites)	http://www.fedstats. gov

Bureau of Census Reports (various reports, filled with all sorts of facts about American life; based on census data collected every 10 years. Look for Census of Population and Housing, The County and City Databook, and USA Counties. Some are on CD-ROM)	http://www.census.gov
Statistical Resources on the Web	http://www.lib.umich.edu/libhome/Documents.center/stats.html
CIA World Fact Book	http://www.odci.gov/cia/publications/factbook/index.html

■ CATALOGS FOR SELECTED LIBRARIES

Look at libraries besides your own to find books to order for interlibrary loan. For further explanation, see the chapter beginning on page 30.

Library of Congress	http://lcweb.loc.gov
New York Public Library	http://www.nypl.org
USA Academic Libraries on the Web	http://sunsite.berkeley.edu/Libweb/usa-acad.html
WWW Virtual Library	http://vlib.org/Overview.html

■ Booksellers and Book Reviewers

To find publishers, use a search engine or try placing the name into a web address (such as www.randomhouse.com).

Amazon.com	http://www.amazon.com
Barnes and Noble	http://www.barnesandnoble.com
Bookzone	http://www.bookzone.com
Great Books	http://www.greatbooks.org
List of Best Books	http://www.tjm.org/books/index.htm
New York Times Book Reviews	http://www.nytimes.com./books

■ E-Texts (online copies of books, magazines, and newspapers)

For an explanation of electronic texts and full-text databases, see the chapter beginning on page 30.

BOOKS ONLINE AND CATALOGS OF E-TEXTS

Alex Catalog of Electronic Texts	http://sunsite.berkeley.edu/alex

Banned Books Online	http://www.cs. cmu.edu/People/ spok/banned-books. html
Books Online	http://digital.library. upenn.edu/books
Carrie: Full-Text Library	http://www.ukans. edu/carrie/carrie_ main.html
Cyberstacks	http://www.public. iastate.edu/ ~CYBERSTACKS
The English Server	http://english-www. hss.cmu.edu/books
ElectricBook	http://www. electricbook.com
The Eris Project	gopher://gopher.vt. edu:10010/10/33
Fulltext Books	http://www.nap. edu/readingroom
Internet Public Library	http://ipl.org/ reading
Internet Wiretap Connection	gopher://wiretap. spies.com/11/books
Omnivore	http://way.net/ omnivore/index.html
Online Books Page	http://www.cs.cmu. edu/Web/books.html
Project Bartleby	http://www.cc. columbia.edu/acis/ bartleby/index.html
Project Gutenberg	http://promo.net/pg

Robert Stockton's Home Page	http://www.cs.cmu. edu/afs/cs.cmu.edu/ user/rgs/mosaic/ rgs-home.html
SUNET'S Index of Classic Library Works	http://ftp.sunet.se/ ftp/pub/etext/ wiretap-classic-library/

JOURNALS AND NEWSPAPERS ONLINE

Almost all print publications now have a website, if only to advertise. If you can't find the address listed here, use a search engine or directory, or try a brief form of the title—such as www.wsj.com, for the *Wall Street Journal,* available for a fee.

Note that most journals and newspapers post only part of the current issue, which may be just what you need if your topic is in this week's news.

AJR Newslink	http://ajr.newslink. org/daym.html
Christian Science Monitor (complete issues since 1980)	http://www. csmonitor.com
E & P Media Links	http://emedia1. mediainfo.com/ emedia
Electronic Journals	http://gateway. library.uiuc.edu/ resource/elinks.asp
Lexis-Nexis (for a fee)	http://www. lexisnexis.com
Los Angeles Times	http://www. latimes.com

New York Times	http://www.nytimes.com
Newsday	http://www.newsday.com
Newspaper Archives	http://metalab.unc.edu/slanews/internet/archives.html
Newspapers Online (links to newspapers all over the world)	http://www.mediainfo.com/edpub/e-papers.home.page.html
News Resources	http://cybereditions.com/aldaily
Newsweek	http://www.newsweek.com
Online Magazines	http://www.pathfinder.com
Salon	http://www.salon.com
Selected Electronic Journals	http://www.library.uiuc.edu/edx/uiucejrn.htm
Slate	http://www.slate.com
Total News (links to local and national newspapers)	http://www.totalnews.com
University of Houston Library *(Scholarly Journals Distributed Through the Web)*	http://info.lib.uh.edu/wj/letters.htm
USNews Online *(U.S. News and World Report)*	http://www.usnews.com/usnews/home.htm

| *Washington Post* | http://www.washingtonpost.com |
| *Wired* | http://www.wired.com |

■ SEARCH TOOLS FOR DISCUSSION GROUPS

For an explanation of discussion groups, see the chapter beginning on page 34.

This list includes routes to information about real-time (synchronous) typed conversations (IRC, chat rooms, MUDS, MOOs) as well as about mailing lists, bulletin boards, newsgroups, Usenet, and other asynchronous discussion groups (where you can read and send messages at your convenience).

To Retrieve Threads of Conversation from Previous Discussions (recommended for research purposes)

| *Deja* | http://www.deja.com |
| *AltaVista* | http://www.altavista.com |

To Find Scholarly and Professional E-Conferences

http://n2h2.com/KOVACS

To Find ListServs or Newsgroups by Subject

CataList: the Official Catalog of Listserv Lists — http://www.listserv.net/lists/listref.html

Liszt, the Mailing List Directory — http://www.liszt.com

OneList — http://onelist.com

Publicly Accessible Mailing Lists — http://www.neosoft.com/internet/paml

Tile.Net/Listserv — http://www.tile.net/lists

FAQs for Usenet Groups — http://www.cis.ohio-state.edu/hypertext/faq/usenet/top.html

Online Chat Resources — http://www.predawnia.org

■ ADDRESSES FOR QUERY BY E-MAIL

For an explanation of sending a query by e-mail, see the chapter beginning on page 39.

Note: Unlike phone directories, directories of Internet addresses can be very uneven: they do not include everyone who would like to be listed, and people who don't want to be listed change their address as soon as it is posted. Although Lycos and Yahoo have very large databases, you may have to make a phone call or e-mail a friend to get the e-mail address of someone you want to query.

Lycos People Finder — http://www.whowhere.lycos.com

Yahoo People Search	http://www.yahoo.com/search/people

■ DIRECTORIES

Directories on the Web

BigBook (yellow pages of the Internet)	http://www.bigbook.com
BigFoot (compendium of all the telephone directories in the U.S.)	http://www.bigfoot.com
Switchboard (white pages)	http://www.switchboard.com
Yellowwweb Pages	http://www.yellowwweb.com

Directories in the Library, on CD-ROM

Some of these are available to some library subscribers from home.

Dun's Business Locator

Dun's Small Business Sourcing File

Encyclopedia of Associations (lists addresses of professional associations)

Foundation Directory (lists addresses of philanthropies and specialized studies)

Net Phone

Standard and Poor's Corporations

■ ASK AN EXPERT

The addresses listed below are for sites where the experts are available for answering your question. In addition, check the archives for *Talk of the Nation* <http://www.npr.org>, National Public Radio's talk show that includes world-renowned experts. On *Talk of the Nation Science Friday* <www.sciencefriday.com>, the experts are all scientists; the roster has included a significant number of nobel laureates.

When you type a question into a query box, the answers are usually instantaneous but not personalized. When you send an e-mail, allow up to a week for a response, but it will usually be tailored to your question.

AltaVista	http://www.altavista.com
Ask an Expert Sources	http://www.cln.org/int_expert.html
Ask Jeeves	http://www.ask.com
Last-Word: Answers to Kids' Questions	http://www.last-word.com
Scientific American Ask the Experts	http://www.sciam.com/askexpert/index.html

■ GOPHER

Many Gopher sites are active but no longer updated. However they can still provide valuable information. For further explanation, see page 42.

Galaxy (links to a large number of gopher sites)	http://www.einet.net

Gopher Directory	gopher://gopher.ed.gov/1
University of Minnesota Gopher	gopher://gopher.tc.umn.edu

■ TELNET

Telnet sites are not easy to use, but some libraries and discussion groups are only accessible via Telnet. For further explanation, see page 42.

Galaxy	http://www.einet.net

(links to a large number of Telnet sites)

■ OTHER HELPFUL SITES FOR RESEARCH

American Civil Liberties Union	http://www.aclu.org
Artcyclopedia	http://www.artcyclopedia.com
Center for Responsive Politics	http://www.crp.org
Electronic Zoo	http://www.avma.org/ezoo
Environment	http://www.earthwatch.org
FAIR (Fairness and Accuracy in Reporting)	http://www.fair.org
High Tech Urban Legends	http://kumite.com/myths

How Stuff Works	http://www.howstuffworks.com
Internet Movie Database	http://www.imdb.com
JobWeb (job listings)	http://www.jobweb.com
Kim Komando (computer and Internet expert)	http://www.komando.com
Library of Congress's American Memory Site (mulitmedia archives)	http://memory.loc.gov/ammem/amhome.html
Louvre Museum (in France)	http://www.mistral.culture.fr/louvre
National Public Radio	http://www.npr.org
Online Archive of California	http://www.oac.cdlib.org
Public Broadcasting System	http://www.pbs.org
Science Friday (conversations with scientists on National Public Radio)	http://www.scifri.com
Smithsonian Institution	http://www.si.edu
Urban Legends	http://www.snopes.com/spoons/faxlore/mydek.htm
WebMuseum	http://www.netspot.unisa.edu.au/wm
Women's Heritage	http://www.womensheritage.org

■ FREE CLIPART

A+ Art   http://www.aplusart.com

Barry's Clip Art Server   http://www.barrysclipart.com

Noetic Art   http://www.noeticart.com

■ HELP WITH STYLE, GRAMMAR, AND USAGE

Jack Lynch's Page
(grammar and style
notes)   http://andromeda.rutgers.edu/~jlynch/writing

OWL
(Online Writing Lab
at Purdue University)   http://www.owl.trc.purdue.edu/prose.html

A Punctuation Miscellany   http://www.fas.harvard.edu/~wricntr/comma.html

University of Maine
(links to other writing
centers)   http://www.ume.maine.edu/~wcenter/others.html

The Word Monger
(online newsletter
addressing issues of
writing professionally)   http://www.alexcommunications.com/newsletter.htm#TOP

Writer's Block
(online newsletter
addressing issues of
writing professionally)   http://www.niva.com/originalwritblok/index.htm

Help with Designing Electronic Documents

Bobby
(a free service that checks a website's accessibility for people with disabilities)

http://www./cast.org/bobby

Lynch and Horton's Web Style Guide

http://info.med.yale.edu/caim/manual/contents.html

Web Design Virtual Library

http://www.wdvl.com

WWWConsortium

http://www.w3.org

Help with Details for Publishing and Documenting Research

Note: On its website, ACS does not give information about how to document. However, you can see samples in the reference pages of the publications there. At all the sites listed you will get information about the publications that will give the very specific requirements for the respective disciplines.

ACS [American Chemical Society]. Provides the format used by courses and publications in chemistry—used also in mathematics and physics

http://www.acs.org

APA [The American Psychological Association]. Provides the format used by publications in the social sciences	http://www.apa.org/journals/webref.html
CBE [Council of Biology Editors]. Provides rules for two styles—the author-date system, similar to the APA style, and the numbered reference system presented in this book	http:// www.cbe.org.cbe
The Chicago Manual of Style. Provides guidelines for most professional publications. Follow this style if you are not bound by the requirements of a particular discipline	http://www.press.uchicago.edu/Misc/Chicago/cmosfaq.html
The Columbia Guide to Online Style. Provides guidelines for documenting electronically retrieved sources, for papers in either the humanities or the sciences	http://columbia.edu/cu/cup/cgos/idx_basic.html
MLA [Modern Language Association] Provides the details for format in papers for courses in English, film, literature, and the study of foreign languages	http://www.mla.org
Web Sources to Convert Journal Titles into Abbreviations. Provides links to sites where you can enter the title of a	http://www.lib.uoguelph.ca/Training/Users/LibEd/convert_journal_title_abbreviati.htm

journal and get its
appropriate abbreviation
for CBE and ACS styles,
or enter an abbreviation
found in an index to get
the full title of the journal,
which must be listed in
all other styles

■ Help With Foreign Languages

Computerized translations remain problematical;
usually checking with a native speaker afterward is
essential. Be aware that websites you find via
searching for "English as a second language" are
often class projects created by students, and they
may not have been corrected by the teacher.
Double check with your textbook and your writing
center. If you need to practice your language skills,
a discussion group in that language is often an
ideal place.

Babelfish
(allows you to request a
translation of a phrase,
a message, or contents
of an entire website)

http://www.
babelfish.altavista.
digital.com

Travlang
(translating dictionaries)

http://dictionaries.
travlang.com

■ Dictionaries

*Dictionary of American
Regional English*

http://polyglot.lss.
wisc.edu/dare/
dare.html

*Merriam-Webster
Dictionary*

http://www.
m-w.com

Roget's Thesaurus	http://www.thesaurus.com
A Web of Online Dictionaries	http://www.facstaf.bucknell.edu/rbeard/diction.html

■ ENCYCLOPEDIAS

Encyclopedia Britannica (on CD-ROM or online; the most definitive comprehensive encyclopedia)	http://www.eblast.com http://www.britannica.com
Free Internet Encyclopedia	http://clever.net/cam/encyclopedia.html

■ QUOTATIONS ORGANIZED BY SUBJECT

Bartlett's Familiar Quotations	http://www.columbia.edu/acis/bartleby/bartlett
The Quotations Page	http://www.starlingtech.com/quotes

■ FREE E-MAIL ACCOUNTS

These accounts (paid for by advertising) have the advantage of being accessible from any computer with access to the Web. Although at times slow, they are a nice backup to accounts through your local library, college, or business—especially when you are traveling.

Just click on the "free E-mail" button on the homepage of most search engines listed on page 171 or at one of these websites:

http://www.eudora.com

http://www.hotmail.com

http://www.juno.com

INDEX